BMW M-series

BMW M-series
Including M1, M3, M5, M635 and M Roadster

A collector's guide
by Chris Rees

MOTOR RACING PUBLICATIONS LTD
Unit 6, The Pilton Estate, 46 Pitlake, Croydon CR0 3RY, England

First published 1997

British Library Cataloguing in Publication Data

Rees, Chris
   BMW M-series : a collector's guide
   1. BMW automobile – Collectors and collecting cars – Collectors and collecting
   I. Title
   629.2'222

ISBN 1-899870-18-0

Printed in Great Britain by
The Amadeus Press Ltd
Huddersfield, West Yorkshire

Contents

The 3 Series has been at the heart of BMW's M success story. Here a quintet of E30 and E36 models, displaying saloon, coupe and convertible body styles, are paraded alongside the car which anticipated the concept – the short-lived BMW 2002 Turbo.

Introduction

If the story of BMW in recent times is one of inexorable rise, then one should naturally be drawn by what is regarded as the pinnacle of its achievements. There is little doubt that the division known as M has a status within and without BMW as the highest expression of the BMW philosophy, 'the ultimate driving machine'. Drivers aspire to experience the M legend, BMW employees yearn to work for it, and writers exhaust their supply of superlatives in describing it.

M stands for Motorsport. Since 1972, Motorsport has been a separate company-within-a-company. Nominally, its primary function is to advance the cause of BMW's competitions effort – a course in which it has been phenomenally successful – but its other main brief is to develop, and sometimes to manufacture, high-performance and high-specification road cars.

In BMW's phraseology, M is 'the most powerful letter in the world', for the application of the tri-coloured 'M' badge means that something exceptional has happened. BMW's M division has endorsed a product honed in its hallowed workshops and test tracks and passed it as worthy of its mark. Such cars are not aftermarket specials, they are proper BMW cars, yet they do not fall into the same category as other BMWs, or indeed any other category. M cars are utterly unique, as I hope the story told in this book will convey.

Acknowledgements

I would like to acknowledge the invaluable help and support of everyone who thought it worthwhile to sacrifice their time and invest the effort required to make this book as accurate and as complete as possible. Special thanks are due to Alun Parry and Chris Willows at BMW (GB) for all their effort, diligence and friendliness. In Germany, I would like to thank Friedbert Holz in the Motorsport press department, Alexander Hildebrandt for his work on the production figures, Eva-Maria Burkhardt for researching competition results, and Heinrich Klebl of BMW Tradition for making the best of a difficult situation at BMW Historical Archives.

On the photographic side, I would like again to acknowledge the efforts of BMW in Britain and in Germany to supply images. A large debt of gratitude must also be extended to Tim Hignett and his senior executives Simon Crompton and Toby Partridge at BMW dealership L&C, of Tunbridge Wells and Croydon, for their sterling efforts in making available several delectable M Series models from L&C's classic car collection for photographic purposes.

Finally, I must pay tribute to the patience and persistence of John Blunsden, my publisher, who was also forced to bring his camera to the rescue at short notice.

June 1996   Chris Rees

BMW's competition successes stretch right back to 1929, when a team of three drivers (Koeppen, Kandl and Wagner) won the International Alpine rally. The successful model was the 3/15, BMW's version of the Austin Seven, which it made until 1933.

By 1938, the BMW 328 was becoming the car to beat in international competition. Here at the Nürburgring, 328s almost fill the starting grid for a 2-litre sportscar race supporting the 1938 German GP. The winner, in car No 10, was Paul Greifzu, who averaged 75.7mph.

CHAPTER 1

The heritage of BMW Motorsport

The true meaning of a letter

Motorsport, in the strict sense of the term, is part of the lifeblood of BMW. Over a period of many years, the company has enjoyed some spectacular successes through a wide-ranging series of competition programmes which have involved everything from Formula 1 to a variety of classes of production car racing and rallying.

But in the phraseology of BMW's current perspectives, the word Motorsport has far greater connotations than this. Its wider meaning harks back to the days before BMW went racing, when Mercedes-Benz was always the dependable name, but BMW meant something altogether more incisive, more stimulating – the enthusiast's choice. More recently, the word Motorsport has come to symbolize the very essence of what makes a BMW special, extrapolated to the edge of its envelope. No longer merely a moniker for the track, it has a lifeblood of its own, finding expression in tuned, honed and tailored cars for the road.

The inspiration for such an approach can be traced back to the earlier days of BMW car manufacture. Developing a theme established by the company's first postwar product, the expensive 501 'Baroque Angel', from 1954 onwards BMW offered a pair of exciting sportscars, both of them styled by Count Albrecht Goertz. There was the 503, on a standard-wheelbase saloon chassis, and it was followed by the exquisite 507, which was built on a shortened version. Both featured BMW's aluminium V8 engine and were beautifully hand-built, but very expensive machines.

It was not until the arrival of the *Neue Klasse* saloons of the early 1960s that BMW established itself as a producer of popular cars with a sporting slant. The BMW 1500 of 1961 was a convincing, efficient, cleanly-styled saloon – one could say the very essence of what BMW has subsequently become. The larger-engined 1800 and 2000 versions which followed it appealed even more to enthusiasts, the ultimate model, the fuel-injected 2000Tii, being capable of 115mph.

The *Neue Klasse* was joined in 1966 by what has since become known as the '02' range. These more compact two-door saloons were absolute benchmarks as drivers' cars, with entertaining handling and impressive performance. BMW took the opportunity to fit its fuel-injected 130bhp 1,990cc engine into the basic shell to make the seminal 2002tii: 120mph was exceptional for 1971. The ultimate '02' was the 170bhp 2002 Turbo of 1973; early versions even bore the colours of BMW Motorsport. However, despite appearances, this model can be discounted as a significant historical step since it was very short-lived, and subsequently BMW rejected, in the most dogmatic terms, the use of turbocharging as a means of extracting more power from its engines.

Another important model in BMW's line-up was the CS Coupe range launched in 1965, initially with a 2-litre four-cylinder engine, but definitively with silky smooth in-line 'sixes' which were decisive in their performance. Independent tuners Alpina successfully campaigned a 2800CS in the 1969 European Touring Car Championship (ETC), winning two events. Ultimately, the CS and CSL would become totally dominant in ETC racing in the 1970s under the BMW Motorsports banner.

The delicate beauty of Albrecht Goertz's design for the BMW 507 penetrates the decades since it was created in 1955. This was BMW's first true postwar sportscar: V8 power, roadster or coupe styles, and a top speed approaching 140mph. Only 252 were built.

Since 1972, Motorsport has had its own home within BMW, a company-within-a-company. BMW Motorsport GmbH was established in 1972, at first as a nebulous organization responsible for the competitions programme at BMW. It occupied various buildings at BMW's headquarters until, in 1979, a redevelopment of BMW's site at Preussenstrasse, in Munich, gave Motorsport a dedicated HQ of its own, commensurate with its 'company-within-a-company' status.

Fresh from his successes at Ford, where he took the Capri RS to the pinnacle of its achievements in Touring Car racing, the new head of BMW Motorsport GmbH was Jochen Neerpasch. Still very young, he was able to inject the necessary enthusiasm and expertise into the organization to produce a championship-winning machine in the totally dominant CSL of 1973.

A brand new corporate livery was created for the 1973 season: racing CSLs incorporated new coloured stripes in blue, violet and red. The same scheme of stripes abutting a chunky letter 'M' became the corporate identity of BMW

Motorsport: the legend of 'the most powerful letter in the world' had begun. That phrase would become the copywriter's cast-in-stone description of BMW M, right up to the current day.

BMW Motosport's racing and rallying triumphs are detailed fully in Chapter 11, and it is interesting to chart how what was set up as a purely competitions wing of BMW came to encompass so many diverse characteristics. It was perhaps the willingness of the Motorsport division to build special one-off road cars for favoured customers and high-ranking BMW officials which set the whole ball rolling. BMW Motorsport was used to supplying race privateers with the specification they wanted, and it was a small step to apply the same skills to road cars as well.

Already BMW was taking advantage of the carefully branded Motorsport image, and the 1970s saw a proliferation of semi-official 'wings' within the Motorsport division. There was M Power, responsible for Motorsport engines, road or race. M Technics covered technical components like aerodynamic aids, chassis tuning parts,

With the 1972-75 3.0CSL, BMW had not only a handsome and extremely capable sporting Grand Tourer, but also the raw material to launch a successful assault on the race tracks of Europe. The CSL was a homologation special with lightweight aluminium opening panels and plexiglass windows, and only 1,039 of this model were made.

wheels and tyres, and so on. M Team was the racing department, and M Style was the most devolved, offering branded fashion accessories. Some called this cynical marketing, but others recognized the legitimate exploitation of one of the strongest aspects of the BMW organization. Whatever the views, the exercise was certainly successful.

As for the development of a line of M-badged cars for the road, this all started with the M1. BMW wanted to beat Porsche on the track, so in 1975 the company set out to create a mid-engined supercar. As you can read in the following chapter, the M1 never got a chance to challenge Porsche at its own game, but it did go racing, and in order to do this it was necessary to homologate the car. Hence the M1 was offered in road-going form to the public. BMW Motorsport did not actually build the cars (that was a very

complicated story...), but it did make all the mechanical components and it tested every completed car once it had been delivered to the factory. The M1 was an unrepeatable exercise and was probably the last ever BMW supercar.

The company's considerable experience with the then-current 5 Series (most of the special Motorsport one-offs were based on the chunky E12 four-door saloon) led it to create the first of a series of more affordable M-badged road cars – the M535i, first shown in 1979. Production of this model (which was the most sheepishly-clothed of all wolves) remained very limited, but it was historic in so far as it was the first M road car with no direct competition rationale behind it.

After that, of course, BMW M flourished as a brand, principally with the M3, M635CSi and M5. As it grew in

stature and in production volume, the Motorsport site at Preussenstrasse became increasingly cramped, and in 1986 the company moved to a new factory at Garching. In 1993, BMW Motorsport became known simply as BMW M GmbH. It was split into three different units: BMW M Cars, BMW Individual (for tailor-made modifications to cars) and BMW Driver Training (an office for which Motorsport had been reponsible since 1976).

Yet BMW M has never lost sight of its competition roots. It has kept its works programme in full development and, at the time of writing, there is speculation that BMW might even re-enter the world of Formula 1. Meanwhile, BMW maintains the tradition that every motor racing engine it has developed is based on one which has also seen service on the road. As Martin Hainge, the British-born head of sales and marketing at BMW Motorsport in 1992, said: "Lots of people will give you that stuff about how racing improves road cars. Here, it's absolutely true."

As these words were being written, further chapters on the road-going M cars were also taking shape as the next-generation M5 and M-powered Z3 Coupe were being readied for production. Even if M really is the most powerful letter in the world, it looks set to become stronger still in the years ahead.

The famous tricolour stripes of BMW Motorsport were clearly in evidence on the controversial 1973 2002 Turbo. This car can perhaps be viewed as a prototype M car: BMW took a standard production saloon and gave it more power, an enhanced chassis and cosmetic tweaks. The model's short life and rarity (only 1,672 were built) is explained by the timing of its launch: in the middle of the OPEC oil crisis.

CHAPTER 2

The exotic M1

BMW's short-lived supercar – 1978-81

Jochen Neerpasch was the man who was responsible for the birth of BMW's only production supercar. BMW's audacious Motorsport manager wanted a car to take over the racing mantle of the highly successful CSL, to create a car which could do battle with Porsche in the World Sports Car Championship and could win at Le Mans. Unlike the CSL, its successor would not be a front-engined car, but a radically different machine: it evolved as the mid-engined M1.

In some respects, the M1 can be traced back as far as 1972, when BMW's head of design, Frenchman Paul Bracq, designed the BMW Turbo. This mid-engined coupe may have been a mere show car, with active and passive safety as its main *raisons d'etre*, but it was designed to be entirely practical in use. Indeed, BMW stated at the time that it was conceived "with a view to making the car a feasible proposition for series production". Notable features were anti-lock brakes, a suprisingly practical interior layout, gullwing doors and a turbocharged 2-litre engine sited – significantly – aft of the seats.

Perhaps this was in Neerpasch's mind when he embarked on his odyssey to produce a mid-engined supercar in 1975. The initial plan called for a Group 5 'Silhouette' racer capable of winning Le Mans, but homologation rule changes would scotch the M1's chances in this respect: BMW was forced to abandon its Group 5 plans because the sport's governing body insisted that the required minimum of 400 cars should be built before the model could go racing. In the event, the racing M1 would conform instead to Group 4 regulations.

BMW did not have the spare capacity to contemplate building such a specialized car in the quantities required to homologate it, so it sought a partner to undertake the construction of prototypes and then to manufacture the cars. Neerpasch selected Lamborghini as that partner.

Lamborghini had secured some £1.1 million of funding from the Italian government, and this cash injection gave BMW the confidence to signal the go-ahead for the Sant'Agata firm to build a series of prototypes, with the intention that it would make the bodies and construct the finished cars, using mechanical components imported from Germany. In that bullish climate, the intended homologation production run was planned to be as high as 800. Neerpasch scheduled for a show debut at Geneva in March 1978, with the car's first race to be Le Mans later the same year.

Lamborghini began work on the car, and several prototypes were seen running around its Sant'Agata works in Bologna from the summer of 1977, when the first prototype became a runner. Although reports in the press referred to the car as the BMW 835, BMW initially referred to it by its factory type designation E26. However, soon it was confirmed that the car was to be called M1 – the historic first use of the letter 'M' to denote Motorsport on a road car.

Giorgetto Giugiaro, of Ital Design, had been contracted to design the M1's bodywork. His interpretation of the mid-engined supercar was typically clean and it aged extremely

Designer Paul Bracq's BMW Turbo of 1972 might be regarded as the ancestor of the M1, since it was a mid-engined road car with a 280bhp engine and a surprisingly practical layout. However, it was only ever intended as a show car, demonstrating BMW's commitment to safety features.

well. Less curvaceous than Ferraris of the period, it struck the right chord with BMW.

Of course, it incorporated the BMW kidney grille, but new to BMW were such ideas as pop-up headlamps, slats over the rear window and flying rear buttresses. Aerodynamically, the design was nothing special – the drag coefficient was around 0.40, said BMW. However, BMW claimed that the car's centre of pressure, and therefore its balance, remained constant whatever the speed, hence the only aerodynamic aid fitted was a small wraparound front spoiler.

Airflow was also cleverly arranged. Grilles at the front allowed air to cool the front-mounted radiator, the warm air exiting through louvres in the front lid. Air for the engine was sucked in through apertures in the recesses for the rear quarter-lights, and came up through louvres in the engine bay lid and out through slatted panels on the rear haunches. Small scoops in front of the windscreen supplied air to the interior.

The Lamborghini-designed chassis was a very strong square-section steel-tube spaceframe, which was panelled where necessary with sheet steel and had superstructures in round tubular steel. The glassfibre bodywork which clothed it was totally unstressed.

Mechanically, BMW had made tentative plans to develop a 4-litre V12 engine, which could have been ideal for the M1, but in the event, BMW turned to its experience with the M88 CSL Group 2 six-cylinder engine. This had a capacity of 3,453cc, and the piston bores were siamesed. Most importantly, in the M1's cylinder head the chain-driven double overhead camshafts operated four valves per cylinder, with large inlet and exhaust valves and 'hot' timing. Other changes were a stronger forged steel crankshaft, longer connecting rods, different pistons, dry-sump lubrication, Marelli electronic ignition and Kugelfischer/Bosch fuel injection. With a mere 9:1 compression ratio, a maximum output of 277bhp at 6,500rpm was achieved, and peak torque was 239lb.ft at 5,000rpm. To let everyone know this was the product of BMW's dedicated Motorsport department, the ribbed head

The primary purpose of the M1 at its conception was to go racing, even though fate and circumstance would eventually drastically alter its race career. BMW presented its new M1 as the fastest-ever BMW; it was launched exactly 50 years after the company's first car, the Dixi.

Photographed more than 18 years after it first went on the road, this M1 could easily pass for a supercar of the Nineties. Rearward vision from the driver's seat leaves something to be desired, although it is not as restricted as this view of the slatted rear quarters might suggest.

Lamborghini designed the tough spaceframe chassis, which was tremendously effective and compares well with the best-handling cars of today. Lamborghini was also meant to manufacture the M1, but the deal went sour, resulting in one of the most complicated manufacturing processes ever seen. The glassfibre bodywork was completely unstressed.

The heart of the M1 was its engine, a development of the six-cylinder unit used in the racing CSL. With a capacity of 3,453cc, a 24-valve cylinder head, twin overhead camshafts and an output of 277bhp, this was a well-known, reliable and efficient power unit. This basic engine powered a whole generation of future M cars.

The M1 is rightly regarded as a design classic. Airflow management was clever and efficient: air entered the engine bay via ducting behind the rear quarter-window (which opened to allow the rear window to be cleaned) and exited through black slats above the rear wheels.

covers carried 'BMW Motorsport' script.

The drivetrain was mounted in a conventional in-line format, which made it longer than Ferrari's engine-over-gearbox layout, but weight distribution was a very balanced 44/56 front/rear and the engine was sited very low down to make the centre of gravity as low as possible. A ZF five-speed indirect transaxle was used in conjunction with a Fichtel & Sachs twin-plate clutch and a 40 per cent limited-slip differential. The gear lever gate imitated racing practice with a dogleg first.

Lamborghini's main input was in the suspension department, courtesy of the efforts of Gianpaolo Dallara. Fully adjustable unequal-length wishbones front and rear were fitted with alloy hubs, coil springs, telescopic dampers and anti-roll bars at both ends. Pronounced anti-dive/anti-squat geometry was designed-in. Road cars would be fitted with a new design of Campagnolo alloy wheel: 7x16in front and 8x16in rear, shod with 205/55 and 225/50 VR16 Pirelli P7 tyres. Braking was achieved by sizeable ventilated discs at the front (300mm/11.8in) and inboard discs

(297mm/11.7in) at the rear, servo-assisted of course.

Inside the car, BMW's no-nonsense approach was very evident. Much of the switchgear and instrumentation was taken from standard production BMWs (notably the 6 Series) and the overall air was almost sober, thanks to the exclusive use of grey and black materials. A hooded binnacle contained all the major dials and controls: a 9,000rpm rev-counter, 280kmh speedometer, minor gauges for oil temperature, oil pressure, water temperature and fuel level, plus warning lights, heating and ventilation controls. The flat three-spoke Motorsport steering wheel was adjustable for reach, but the driving position was dictated by the offset positioning of the pedals. There was little space for luggage: since the front end was occupied by the radiator, brake servos and fuel injection computer, everything had to go into a compartment behind the engine.

Standard equipment included air conditioning, a heated rear window, electric windows, remotely-operated door mirrors, opening rear quarter-lights, leather-edged Recaro seats and rear foglights. The pop-up headlamps were

17

electrically-operated, rising on full beam only, the grille-mounted foglamps being used for flashing.

After much press speculation concerning the Lamborghini deal, BMW formally announced in April 1978: "Unhappily, BMW find themselves forced to terminate the agreement in order not to endanger the M1 project." This curt press release alluded to the huge problems the Lamborghini connection had run into; by this stage, work was already well behind schedule. Seven prototypes had been built, but Lamborghini had not delivered the promised batch of pilot-build cars, which should have been ready in March. And it was certainly in no position to manufacture M1s at the agreed rate of two per week.

Lamborghini's finances were in a parlous state. It had spent all its government money and was frankly broke, unable to buy the components needed to begin production. The whole company was even offered for sale to BMW, but the German firm would not consider it; it had already spent a lot of money on the M1 project and was in no mood to take on a firm which was likely to drain more of its resources. This was perhaps the beginning of the end for Jochen Neerpasch within BMW, since he was reportedly keen to see his brainchild through with Lamborghini.

The M1 project now looked shaky, but BMW had committed itself financially. In addition, the M1's future looked more promising since FOCA's Max Mosley – mindful of BMW's awkward position now that homologation rules had changed – agreed with Neerpasch to run a Procar series for M1 racers at Formula 1 Grand Prix meetings (see Chapter 11 for the full story of the M1's racing career).

Therefore BMW steamed ahead. The job of assembling the M1 was transferred to Baur, in Stuttgart, which was already building the 3 Series Cabriolet for BMW. Yet ironically, much of the car was still manufactured in Italy, in one of the most convoluted manufacturing processes ever known. The moulds for the glassfibre production bodies, which had been conceived by Ital Design, were used by Trasformazione Italiana Resina to make M1 bodies (there were 10 mouldings in each body). The chassis and

Considering its supercar status, the M1's interior was surprisingly easy to live with and utterly devoid of gimmicks and 'flash', although the level of equipment was high. Many of the controls came from other BMW models. All examples of the M1 were left-hand drive.

The shallow front compartment of the M1's glassfibre body is largely filled by the ducting for the large radiator, the battery and attendant box of electrics, the fluid reservoir connected to the brake master-cylinder and, on the extreme left, the screen washer supply tank.

Mid-engined supercars generally have little claim to much luggage capacity, and the M1 was no exception. Despite the insulation, the boot became very hot on a long run, which impinged on its effectiveness still further.

suspension jigs were kept at Modena by the Marchesi brothers, who built the spaceframes and sent them to Ital Design, in Turin, which then bonded and riveted the bodies to the chassis and sprayed and glazed them. From there, completed body/chassis units were despatched to Baur for the installation of all mechanical and trim components – engines from BMW, transaxles from ZF, plus interiors. Finally, each M1 was tuned, checked and road-tested by BMW Motorsport in Munich.

As well as road versions, BMW offered Group 4 racers for sale to the public at a cost some 50 per cent higher. A total of 60 of these M1 racers were delivered, including the Procar examples. The Group 4 M1 specification included a much-modified version of the 3.5-litre 24-valve fuel-injected BMW 'six'. Output was 470bhp at 9,000rpm and 282lb.ft of torque at 7,000rpm. BMW quoted a 0-62mph time of 4.5 seconds and claimed that its maximum speed was 192mph.

The Group 4 car was shown with aluminium centre-lock hubs and very wide wheels, shod with 10 x 16in front and 12.5 x 16in rear tyres, which naturally needed fatter arches to cover them. Other bodywork modifications included a deep front spoiler; the original machine, as pictured in the first press shots, had no rear spoiler, but one was fitted for its first races. A full rollcage was also required.

Bearing in mind that the road M1 weighed a quite considerable 1,440kg (3,175lb), performance was better than might have been expected. BMW claimed a top speed of 161mph (260kmh) and some testers even exceeded this. BMW's claim of 0-62mph in 6.5 seconds was also quite conservative, since *Autocar* magazine managed to hustle one to 60mph in just 5.5 seconds, comfortably quicker than any of its supercar rivals.

Responsiveness was exceptional for a six-cylinder engine.

John Miles, writing in *Autocar*, commented in his test report that the M1 was "a beautifully responsive and sometimes thrilling motor car... The throttle operates beautifully smoothly, and the engine responds beautifully to it at all times... Once warm the M1 asks to be driven hard for hours on end... Perhaps the car's greatest joy is being able to consistently use its huge reserves of power to rocket out of corners, and past others."

Praise was lavished on the M1's finely weighted, accurate and unassisted steering, phenomenal grip, confident and broadly neutral cornering characteristics in dry conditions, superb brakes, surprisingly accomplished ride, unexpected 20mpg economy, sensible interior and an overall build quality, which embarrassed every other supercar.

Criticisms were few. It was a noisy beast, but since the sound was so pleasing this was hardly a complaint. More serious perhaps was a tendency for the rear end to break away in the wet, but the limits of adhesion were always quite high. There was some wander in cross winds and the typical mid-engined complaint of poor rear visibility persisted. Headroom was limited, and the seats didn't move very far back and were rather upright. At least there was a small but usable boot behind the engine, but it was obstructed by the spare wheel (a space-saver, but still obtrusive) and since the exhaust sat directly beneath it, heat was a problem.

The life of the M1 was short but sweet. Its public debut was the October 1978 Paris Salon, but the car had already been widely pictured in the press and had gained a lot of advance coverage due to the collapsed Lamborghini deal – BMW board members must surely have been consoling themselves with the old aphorism that all publicity is good publicity.

Sales did not begin until February 1979, a full year behind the intended launch date. The German price was exactly DM100,000 (twice the price of a 635CSi), and this went up to DM113,000 from July 1979 and reached DM144,000 in 1980 (which equated to about £37,500). That was extremely expensive compared with anything else: for instance, a Ferrari 512BB cost £35,100 and a Porsche 3.3 Turbo was £27,950. British customers could only purchase an M1 on a personal import basis, and in left-hand-drive form only. The warranty was also exceptionally short: just six months or 6,000 miles.

But this was an exceptional car produced in tiny numbers. *Autocar* called it "possibly the best mid-engined road car yet". It was exceptionally fast and well-mannered, practical and well-built for a supercar, decidedly unprone to tantrums and remarkably free of major vices. It was a true BMW of supercars.

Production ended in July 1981, after a total of 450 cars had been built. Of those, just under 400 were road cars, the remainder being racers. Today, they are undoubtedly underrated by the general population, but passionately appreciated by the few who are fortunate enough to own one. The M1 was a unique project in BMW's history and one which almost certainly will never be repeated. However, BMW's supercar interest did not die, it merely transformed: the company was to become a very keen participant in the development of the McLaren F1, for which BMW Motorsport designed and built the fabulous V12 engine – a story which is told in Chapter 10.

The M1 was a very expensive car, comfortably exceeding the prices of its rivals. Its customers included racing drivers, royalty and wealthy enthusiasts, and it remains a rare and sought-after machine today.

CHAPTER 3

The classic M3 (E30)

An M car for the people – 1985-91

To the M3 goes the distinction of bringing the M badge to a genuinely broad audience. Unlike the lukewarm 1984 M535i, the M3 was a proper Motorsport-engineered and modified car, which brought new levels of performance to buyers, who did not have to lay their hands on the small fortune asked for an M5 or an M635CSi.

For BMW, the new M3 brought two significant benefits. Firstly, it was a very popular car and it proved satisfyingly profitable. Secondly, it provided an ideal basis for competition, as its brilliant successes in European and World Championship racing would prove.

The need for a high-volume M product was pressing because, in order to qualify for Group A under FISA regulations, a minimum of 5,000 units was required within the first 12 months of production. Obviously, the highly specialized M635CSi would take years to reach this sort of production total. Therefore, using the BMW E30 3 Series – introduced in 1982 – as a basis for a Group A competition car looked to be a compelling idea.

The groundwork for a Group A car based on the forthcoming 3 Series kicked off in the summer of 1981, when a project led by Werner Frowein oversaw the development of a lightweight four-cylinder engine with 16 valves. The iron block of the familiar BMW slant-four engine – which dated from 1961 but was still in use in Formula 2 – was mated to a modified M1/M635 twin-cam four-valves-per-cylinder head. It was modified simply by chopping off the end of the six-cylinder head and blocking the coolant passages!

Thus the internal dimensions of the engine and the layout of the head were shared with the M1, but the four-cylinder format was much more suited to the smaller M3. Its size and weight were kept down, helping both handling and straight-line performance. At the same time, all the benefits of a tried and tested engine remained, while a four-cylinder block (with its short crankshaft) was better able to withstand high revs. With an M1-sized bore of 93.4mm, the five-bearing four-cylinder engine became one of the largest-capacity 'fours' in production at 2,302cc.

Other engine design features included siamesed pistons, BMW's renowned Motronic fuel injection, a special cast alloy sump with baffle plates, a separate oil cooler behind the spoiler and duplex chain-driven overhead camshafts. The 2.3-litre M3 engine developed an impressive 200bhp at 6,750rpm, and an equally impressive 176lb.ft of torque at 4,750rpm. BMW had achieved a remarkable 86.8bhp per litre.

By early 1983, preliminary development work had begun on other aspects of the M3 model. Virtually every part of the standard 3 Series was modified to make the new car worthy of its 'M' badge. In particular, the (comparatively un-aerodynamic) bodywork was targeted and some major modifications were effected; indeed, the only panel which was shared with the rest of the 3 Series was the bonnet. The whole bodyshell was altered to allow for the fitment of a rollcage.

The most obvious bodywork changes were the very wide front and rear wings. These were still made of steel, but

The rear view of an M3 was radically different from any other 3 Series model: a more steeply raked bonded-in rear screen with wider pillars, new bootlid with built-in spoiler, a deep rear bumper/valance and of course the M3 badge.

were designed to cope with 10in wide racing rims – and they were certainly more than sufficient for the road car's BBS 7in wide alloy wheels and 205-section tyres. Harder to spot was the fact that the larger rear window was more steeply raked and the boot line raised, all in the interest of aerodynamics (a Cd of 0.33 was recorded). To aid rigidity, both front and rear screens were bonded in place. Apart from the metal wings, the additional modified bodywork addenda were made of SMC plastic, including the entire bootlid/spoiler, the three-piece front bumper/spoiler, the rear bumper and the sills.

Naturally, the suspension also came in for attention. The strut-type front suspension was given completely new geometry and there were thicker front and rear anti-roll bars. At the front, the anti-roll bar had new pivot points outside the spring strut, and there were twin-tube Boge gas-pressurized dampers all round, uprated rear springs and 15-degree raked trailing arms. New stub-axles encased larger wheel bearings taken from the 5 Series, and there were five-stud hubs (other 3 Series models had only four studs).

Braking was commensurate with the M3's performance: the basic package was derived from the 5 Series. That meant large 284mm ventilated discs at the front and solid 250mm discs at the back. Reinforced single-piston calipers and specially tuned Bosch ABS were standard. The steering was also significantly improved with the addition of a power-assisted quick-ratio rack (19.6:1 – equivalent to 3.6 turns of the steering wheel lock-to-lock – compared with

21.4:1, or 4.5 turns, in the 325i).

The gearbox supplier was Getrag, whose five-speed unit had Borg-Warner synchronization. Fifth represented direct drive in this unit (all other 3 Series BMWs had a direct fourth), while first remained the same as for other 3 Series types at 3.72:1; it is easy to see that the new set of ratios allowed for much more enthusiastic gear-changing. To compensate for the lack of an overdriven top gear, the final drive was much higher than on other 3 Series cars at 3.25:1. Also, a special clutch with a bonded lining was fitted.

One quirk of the M3 transmission was its race-style dogleg first gear, designed for optimum fast changes. A ZF multi-plate 25 per cent limited-slip differential was standard. No automatic gearbox was ever offered.

A decision was taken late in the pre-production programme to develop a catalytic converter for the new engine. Unleaded fuel was selling at a discount in Germany, and the 'green' lobby was forcing manufacturers to respond. More significantly, perhaps, the important American and Japanese markets required catalysts. Unfortunately for them, both the power output and the torque of catalyzed engines suffered, but not by much: 195bhp was only 5bhp less than the 'non-cat' engine, and torque of 169lb.ft was only 7lb.ft lower.

There was also some concern from BMW management that the M3's styling was too aggressive, and the debate caused the delay of the M3's press announcement to July 1985. The success of the wild Mercedes-Benz 190E 2.3-16 (a definite rival) may have been persuasive in letting the M3 keep its spoilers and wide wings. Another factor in the car's favour was that Thomas Ammerschlager (ex-Zakspeed and Audi) joined Motorsport in 1985 in charge of the M3 project.

The interior was also given the M make-over. The driver gripped a three-spoke Motorsport steering wheel and sat on multi-adjustable sports seats (which were an option on ordinary 3 Series models). The rear seats were described as 'individual body-contoured'. Other clues that this was a special BMW included a 260kmh (160mph) speedometer, an 8,000rpm rev-counter (red-lined at 7,300rpm), with an oil temperature gauge and a tiny 'M' logo positioned between the main instruments.

Standard equipment included tinted glass and twin electric door mirrors. On the options list were air conditioning, electric windows, electric sunroof, headlamp

Unlike other BMW M cars, the M3 had a four-cylinder engine, but its specification was very special: 2.3 litres was a large capacity for a 'four', and it developed 200bhp – equating to nearly 87bhp per litre, a remarkable figure for a road car engine.

In construction, the M3 engine was a BMW slant-four block mated to a chopped M1-type four-valves-per-cylinder head. Clearly visible are the Motronic fuel injection system, chain-driven double overhead camshafts and a 'BMW M Power' casting.

wash/wipe, on-board computer, leather trim and various stereo systems.

The public got its first taste of the new M3 at the September 1985 Frankfurt motor show, although this was very much a pre-production prototype. Full production did not begin for another year, in September 1986, with the first deliveries following a couple of months later (the price in Germany was DM58,000). Manufacture did not take place at Motorsport's specialized new Garching plant, but at the main BMW factory in Munich, for this was a comparatively high-production model, and therefore beyond Garching's capability of handling. To satisfy FISA homologation rules, 5,000 had to be built in the first year, and BMW built 2,396 in the last few months of 1986, followed by 6,396 units the following year, easily satisfying the rule-makers. This is not to say that the M3 was a mass-

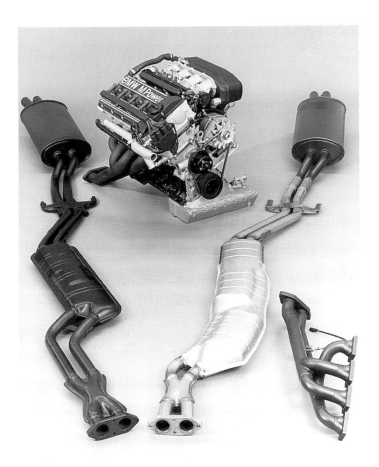

BMW was serious about its environmental reputation and produced a catalyst-equipped version of the M3 engine. Unlike many other engines so equipped, this unit developed only 5bhp less than its non-catalyst equivalent.

produced model: it was always given special treatment within the BMW factory. For example, M3 engines were put together by the same team that made BMW's V12.

Peter Flohr, chairman of BMW M GmbH at the time,

24

Suspension and brakes both came in for attention: front and rear geometry were altered, twin-tube Boge gas dampers were fitted at both ends, the rear wheel bearings came from the 5 Series and brakes were increased in size over the 3 Series.

said of the M3: "This is a sports car within the financial reach of private racing drivers and with sophisticated, but straightforward and unproblematic technical features." BMW added: "The M3 is also the ideal car for the dedicated motorist in search of sheer driving pleasure instead of honours on the race track."

Naturally, performance was the M3's strong suit. BMW claimed a top speed of 146mph and 0-62mph in 6.7 seconds, and testers were able to approach, if not to match, this standard: in the UK, *Autocar* magazine managed 139mph and 0-60mph in 7.1 seconds, while in the United States, the catalyzed M3 scored 143mph and 0-60mph in 7.1 seconds. To soften the effects of heavier fuel

consumption (mpg in the low 20s was usual), an extra 15 litres was added to the capacity of the standard 55-litre tank.

Testers were enthusiastic. They universally praised the sharp throttle response and guttural engine note, the faithful steering feedback and biting turn-in, the phenomenal grip and transformed handling. Yet despite its sharp dynamics, the M3 was also docile in traffic, thanks to its smooth Getrag gearbox, and it rode far better than one might have expected from a car of this nature.

If there was one major criticism, it was the roughness of the four-cylinder engine, which was certainly far less refined than the smooth 'sixes' enjoyed by the next 3 Series models

BMW's fine multi-adjustable front seats made for the ideal driving position. The driver grasped a special Motorsport three-spoke steering wheel.

Unlike other members of the 3 Series family, the rear seats were individually contoured for both rear passengers. The M3 was the perfectly practical performance car.

This view of road and race M3s illustrates how close they were in specification. The engine looks virtually identical, and it is only the reinforced struts, engine top link and revised fluid cylinders which give the game away.

down the chain. Also, the gearbox was judged too notchy by many testers.

Initially, BMW GB was hesitant about importing the new M3, since it was made in left-hand drive only, but there was self-evidently a demand for this car, even in left-hook guise. Therefore, BMW GB began the importation of M3s on a special order basis, the first examples arriving in April 1987 at a hefty cost of £22,750 (over £5,000 more expensive than the top-of-the-range 325i saloon). Despite the cost, some 55 were imported in 1987, followed by 58 in 1988, 62 in 1989 and 36 in 1990 (making a grand total of 211). The USA were also offered the M3 from 1987, in catalyzed 195bhp form, which still made it an extremely rapid car by any standards. Catalyzed M3s had to run on unleaded fuel, whereas the 'non-cat' unit used 98 octane leaded.

Italy was a special market because punishing tax laws there for cars over 2 litres made the M3 uneconomic to sell, so a special model was created for the Italian market only. The so-called 320iS was quite different from the familiar 320i, and can be regarded as a halfway house to an M3. It used a sleeved-down version of the M3 engine, with a bore of 72.65mm for a capacity of 1,990cc. Developing 192bhp (or very nearly 100bhp per litre), it could accelerate from 0-62mph in 7.9 seconds and reach 141mph. However, it shared none of the M3's bodywork modifications, having only front and rear spoilers to distinguish it from other E30 3 Series models. It was also comparatively commonplace: between January 1988 and December 1990 some 3,745 were made.

South African customers were also offered a special semi-M 3 Series, the 333i. This was a joint effort between BMW South Africa, BMW Motorsport and Alpina, and consisted of a standard E30 fitted with a 633CSi 3.3-litre six-cylinder engine. Between 1985 and 1987, some 204 examples of this unusual derivative were produced.

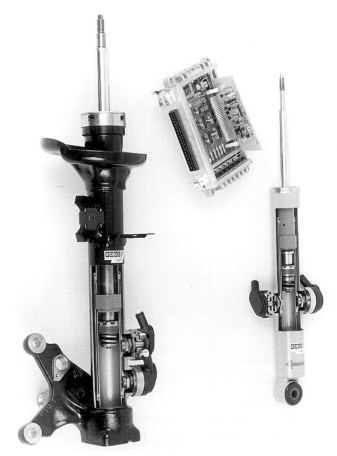

This shot illustrates the control knob for the optional electronic shock absorbers: K means Komfort, N means Normal and S means Sport. Also visible is the dogleg-first shift pattern of the gear lever.

A later option for the M3 was this Electronic Damping Control system from Boge. It had three settings: Sport, Comfort and Normal, intended to give the driver instant adjustability to suit different driving situations.

Changes were few during the M3's short life. Production of non-catalyzed 200bhp engines ended in July 1989, to be replaced in September by a new catalysed unit whose power output had increased to 215bhp; this had first been fitted to the Cecotto/Ravaglia special edition (see below). The engine's cam cover and collector box were now painted in Motorsport colours.

An interesting (but fairly costly) later option was BMW's Electronic Damping Control, sourced from Boge. This offered a choice of three settings for the shock absorbers: Sport, Comfort and a compromise Normal setting in between. If you selected Comfort, it would automatically upgrade to Normal at higher speeds. In truth, there wasn't a great difference between each of the settings, and many customers in the UK found it difficult to justify the EDC option at an extra £1,388.

Evolution I and II

To improve the racing M3's chances on the track, BMW began to homologate improvements to the model on an annual basis, starting as early as February 1987, only a matter of months after M3 production had begun. Each successive Evolution model was sold in a strictly limited edition, just enough to pass homologation rules which required 500 'evolved' road cars.

The first M3 Evolution was hardly an evolution at all. The only changes were aerodynamic: an extended front spoiler and a double-blade rear spoiler, plus a lightweight bootlid. This certainly helped to generate downforce at higher speeds, but it was of almost no practical benefit for road car users. Between February and March 1987, some 505 Evolution M3s were built, of which a mere seven were officially imported to the UK.

The next M3 homologation special arrived in March 1988. The Evolution II embodied a much more ambitious set of modifications. This time the engine received a significant tweak with the addition of a Bosch Motronic chip, new camshafts and pistons, a lightened flywheel, an 11:1 compression ratio and a new air intake tube. The net effect of the changes was a 20bhp boost in output to 220bhp at 6,750rpm, and a small increment of torque to 180lb.ft. The Evo II's final drive also became taller, rising to 3.15:1.

As a result, the Evolution II had a higher maximum speed (152mph instead of 146mph), although the quoted 0-62mph acceleration remained the same at 6.7 seconds. It was also a more tenacious car, thanks to its wider 7.5 x 16in BBS spoked alloy wheels and fatter, lower-profile Pirelli 225/45 ZR tyres.

The Evolution II shared the 1987 evolution's front and double-blade rear spoilers, but these were made of lightweight materials, as were the bootlid, bumper supports, rear screen and rear side windows (giving a total weight saving of 10kg). A graduated tinted windscreen and Motorsport-coloured camshaft cover and air collector completed the picture.

Your choice was between three colours: Macao Blue, Nogaro Silver or Misano Red, all with silver cloth trim and silver leather seat edging. Between March and May 1988, a total of 501 Evolution IIs were built, of which 51 came to the UK with a price tag of £26,960.

The first M3 Evolution model from BMW was a very minor one: the front spoiler jutted out a little further at the bottom, there was a second blade to the rear spoiler and the bootlid was made lighter.

The M3 Cabriolet was the absolute pinnacle of the 3 Series range. It was a pure M3, but had to be modified to suit the convertible bodyshell: hence the standard 3 Series spoiler-less bootlid. It also had the distinction of being exclusively hand-built by BMW Motorsport staff.

M3 Cabriolet

In January 1986, BMW's plant at Regensberg began production of the 3 Series Cabriolet, and it was only a matter of time before an M3 version of this model was developed. The first M3 show cabriolet in fact had a standard 325i engine, coupled to BMW's 4x4 transmission, which had made its debut alongside the M3 saloon at the 1985 Frankfurt show. However, production M3 cabrios would be real M cars, complete with four-cylinder Motorsport engines and rear-wheel drive.

From the nose to the screen, the Cabriolet was pure M3. The convertible roof was shared with the standard 3 Series drop-top, which had no roll-over bar and looked much better for it. This also meant that the M3's raised bootlid could not be fitted, nor the large rear aerofoil; the standard 325i boot spoiler was used instead. The major difference was that the roof was opened and closed electronically, unlike the standard 3 Series model.

BMW's performance claims for the Cabriolet were slightly toned down compared to the saloon because overall weight was 160kg higher at 1,360kg. Top speed dropped by only 1mph, but the 0-62mph sprint took some 0.6 second longer at 7.3 seconds, and that was with the 215bhp version.

Unlike the saloon, production of the drop-top M3 took place at Garching, and every model was hand-built at the works by Motorsport staff. Therefore it was always a highly specialized model with very low production volumes. The first example emerged from the factory gates in May 1988, priced at DM90,000 in Germany. British buyers could order Cabriolets on a strictly limited basis from early 1989 at a daunting price of £37,250 (only 33 were imported over three years, all except one being non-catalyzed).

For the first few months of production, only non-catalyzed (200bhp) cars were made. From October 1988, a 195bhp catalyzed version was also offered, but production of both models was suspended in June 1989. A solitary example of the final batch of these cars was fitted by BMW Motorsport with a 220bhp Evo II engine (chassis number EB85020). Cabriolet manufacture resumed in March 1990 with the more powerful (215bhp) 23 4S 2 engine. Because Cabriolet

The M3 Convertible's roof was electrically operated, and looked as good in the closed as in the open position.

bodyshells continued to be produced after the discontinuation of the saloon in December 1990, the M3 Cabriolet outlived its enclosed sister, the last example leaving the Garching works in July 1991. Just under 800 were made in total.

Although it is not a true M car, it is worth mentioning the special-edition 1990/91 325i Motorsport Cabriolet, which had a definite M Series bias. Based on the six-cylinder 325i convertible, it cost £28,950, of which about £5,000 comprised Motorsport branded items, to wit: an M Technic body kit (front spoiler, side sills and rear skirts), an M Technic uprated suspension and an M Technic steering wheel. A set of 7 x 15in alloy wheels and 205/55 tyres completed the M3-inspired picture.

Other features included an M3-type electro-mechanical hood, standard computer, lined bootlid, blacked-out brightwork and rear panel and colour-coded bumpers and mirrors. Two colours were offered for 1990: Sebring Grey, with black leather upholstery and hood, or Macao Blue, with silver leather upholstery and a blue hood. After a run

of 250 cars in 1990, a further 50 cars were brought into the UK in 1991 with red paint/black hood or blue paint/white hood, both having white leather trim. Automatic transmission was a £1,400 option.

It is also worth mentioning that BMW made a solitary 150mph M3 Touring prototype, details of which were only released after the fact in May 1991. Yet another project was a 3.5-litre six-cylinder M3, using a 315bhp M5 engine, but again this was stillborn, in this case because BMW believed it to be 'simply too fast' for its day.

M3 special editions
Despite the fact that the M3 was undeniably a limited-production model in BMW's wider scheme of things, the Bavarian firm could not resist making a couple of non-Evolution limited-edition versions of the M3.

The first one was called the Europa Meister 88 Celebration, and was designed to take commercial advantage of the M3's victory in the 1988 European Touring Car Championship. It arrived in October 1988 and

BMW launched this special edition M3 in 1989. Called the Roberto Ravaglia in Britain, but known as the Johnny Cecotto elsewhere, it featured a more powerful 215bhp engine (soon to be standardized on regular M3 models). The Evolution-type extended front spoiler can be seen in this picture.

A special striped seat pattern was just one feature of the upgraded interior of the Ravaglia/Cecotto model, each example of which carried a dash plaque signed by the relevant BMW driver.

had the standard catalyzed 195bhp engine, full leather trim, and each one was signed by M3 racer Roberto Ravaglia. A mere 150 were built, and none came to Britain.

The next special-edition M3 followed hot on its heels, in April 1989 (or July 1989 in the UK). This was known by two names, Johnny Cecotto on the continent and Roberto Ravaglia in the UK, each reflecting successful M3 race drivers. This edition boasted a 215bhp three-way catalyzed version of the M3 engine (some five months before the extra power was standarized for the ordinary M3), but its emphasis was more on luxury than the lightweight Evolutions: it boasted bright striped seats with leather

edging and silver treatment for items such as the headlining, dash panel, centre tunnel console and sun visors. Standard equipment included an on-board computer, front electric windows, illuminated gear-knob, wider 7.5x16in wheels with black centres and 225/45 Pirelli P700-Z tyres. Again the double-blade rear spoiler and extended front spoiler were fitted.

Just two body colours were available: Nogaro Silver or Misano Red (this colour even extended to the engine's rocker cover and air collector). Each of the 25 cars brought to the UK, at £26,850 each, was individually signed by Roberto Ravaglia on a plaque inside the car. A total of 505 examples of this special edition were sold worldwide during 1989.

Evolution III Sport

The most exciting M3 of all was saved for last, arriving in December 1989. The third Evolution M3 was far more radically modified than previous incarnations, most significantly relying on an expanded 2.5-litre engine to give

The twin-blade rear spoiler, first seen on the M3 Evolution, was also fitted to the Roberto Ravaglia edition.

The Sport Evo's extra power was telling on the road: top speed rose to 154mph and 0-60mph could be achieved in little over 6 seconds. The lowered suspension and more generous rubber made the handling even more capable: this was now a ruthlessly quick machine.

33

Identifying features of the M3 Sport Evolution include a front spoiler manually adjustable to three different settings. The front bumper is of lightweight construction and the recesses normally occupied by foglights have been converted into brake cooling ducts.

its driver just a little more entertainment when he floored the accelerator.

As ever, the changes were inspired by the need to keep the M3 competitive in the track. The power output of the 2.3-litre engine had gone as high as 322bhp for racing, but that was at a raucous 9,800rpm. An increase in capacity to the 2.5-litre maximum allowed by German and Italian rules was inevitable, and it was achieved by taking the already substantial bore out to 95mm and increasing the throw of the crankshaft to stretch the total capacity to 2,467cc. Other engine changes included bigger inlet valves, sodium-cooled exhaust valves, injection valves to spray cooling oil onto the pistons from beneath and a 282-degree cam. The compression ratio could actually be dropped from 10.5 to 10.2:1.

For racing use (where a slightly larger capacity was used), power output was pushed up to 330bhp at lower revs, but in the road car, the rise in output was proportionately more pronounced: it went up by 18bhp to 238bhp at 7,000rpm. That was within a gasp of 100bhp per litre, a remarkable

achievement for a non-turbocharged road car engine. Torque rose slightly as well.

In practical terms, the extra power meant a top speed of 154mph and 0-62mph in a cracking 6.5 seconds. However, because the final drive was 3.15:1, in place of the standard M3's 3.25:1, the difference in acceleration was not quite as pronounced as it might otherwise have been.

Externally, the most significant change was the adoption of adjustable aerodynamic aids: both front and rear spoilers could be adjusted by virtue of additional flaps on the underside of the front spoiler and on top of the rear one. Both spoilers had a choice of three positions, set simply by undoing soft metal Allen screws. With the spoilers set at their maximum extension, BMW claimed almost zero lift at the front and much increased downforce at the rear. It should also be noted that there were no foglamps in the Evo III's front spoiler, the apertures being used to direct cooling air to the brakes.

A degree of venturi ground effect was engineered in by channelling airflow under the car, creating pressure which

The M3 Sport Evolution's rear spoiler above the lightweight luggage compartment lid is also manually adjustable. The three settings, offering increasing levels of downforce, are designated Monza, Normal and Nurburgring.

literally sucked the car downwards. More aerodynamic work was effected on the front end: the vanes on the BMW kidney grille were reprofiled and rubber inserts were placed in the headlamp mountings, front grille mounts and bonnet surround.

Also, the front wheelarches were expanded so that they could accept 18in diameter wheels for racing (and 7.5x16in road wheels shod with Michelin MXX 225/45 ZR rubber). At the same time, the front suspension was lowered by 10mm and the front brakes benefited from upgraded material.

Inside, the Evo III gained a new three-spoke steering wheel with a scuffed suede rim, the same material also covering the gear-knob (which was illuminated) and the handbrake lever. The anthracite-striped cloth Motorsport front seats were new, too, featuring heavily moulded side supports and apertures in the fixed headrests, which mimicked those for racing harnesses – which could be fitted if you wanted to go onto the track. In the real world, normal red inertia-reel seat belts were fitted, plus new door trim panels and an 'M3' logo on the sills. Otherwise, the interior had a depleted feeling about it, having none of the weight-inducing luxury options such as electric windows, headlamp wash/wipe or air conditioning, though you did get a Motorsport driver's footrest.

The extra weight of the engine was offset by fitting a smaller (62-litre) fuel tank from the 325i, even lighter front and rear bumpers, thinner rear and side glass and no roof grab handles or map lights; kerb weight was therefore kept at 1,200kg.

Better grip for the hands was the reason given for covering the Sport Evo's steering wheel, gear lever and handbrake lever with racing-style suede.

The fact that BMW fitted racing-type seats designed for full harnesses was more for effect than any real possibility that the Sport Evolution III would be raced. Note the vivid striping in the seats and doors.

Two colours were offered for the Evolution III: Jet Black or Brilliant Red, with contrasting bumper inserts. The cost was a whopping £34,500 in Britain, which officially took just 45 out of a total production run of 600, all made between December 1989 and March 1990. Each one had a special individually numbered console-mounted plaque.

Without a doubt, the Evo III was the most desirable of all the original M3 variants. Its bigger engine might have been rougher than 2.3-litre M3 units, but the superior power begged forgiveness for such criticisms. As Richard Bremner commented in *Car* magazine, the Evo III "can be driven hard from the start... It seems to have no quirks, no foibles – just straight ability... This car is a racer in image and a racer in fact." Perhaps most importantly, the Evo III made a feast of all the small but significant details which defined it as the ultimate expression of the E30 M3.

The standard M3 saloon was discontinued in December 1990 in deference to the new E36 3 Series. After a production run of 17,184 M3 saloons of all types, there

When you have it, flout it! There's no reason to be apologetic for having something special beneath the bonnet. In this case M Power stands for a displacement of 2,467cc, a power output of 238bhp at 7,000rpm and torque of 240lb.ft at 4,750rpm.

On the Sport Evolution, the front and rear bumper inserts are finished in a contrasting colour – black on red-painted cars and red when the bodywork is black. These were the only two colour options on this model.

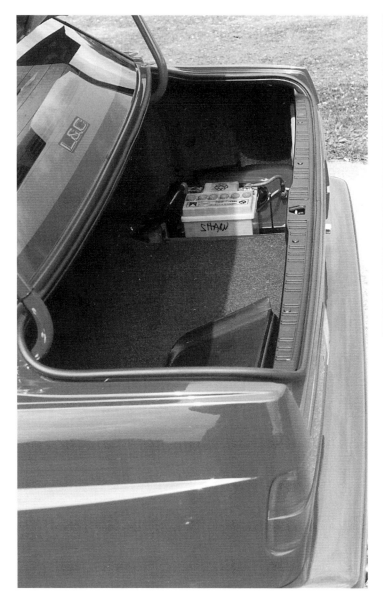

The 16in cross-spoked alloy wheels on the M3 Sport Evolution have 7.5in wide rims and normally carry 225/45 ZR 16 tyres. Not the easiest to clean, perhaps, but they look superb when they have been!

would be a gap of almost two years before the next generation 3 Series would be given the M treatment, although as previously mentioned, the M3 Convertible continued until July 1991. It was the end of a dynasty which is still mourned today.

A little extra weight over the back wheels is often useful on rear-drive cars, and in this instance it is supplied by the battery, seen here with the cover removed.

CHAPTER 4

The smoother M3 (E36)

A new type of supercar – from 1992

When the new E36 3 Series entered production in 1990, it was always on the cards that a Motorsport M3 version would be developed. However, it was also natural that the Garching engineers should wait for the Coupe version of the 3 Series to arrive, since this was the obvious basis for a new M3. The standard Coupe was launched in January 1992, and by April details began filtering out about the new M3 Coupe.

The E36 BMW 3 Series was a much bigger car in all dimensions than the previous generation, and was significantly heavier as a result. It was evident that the direction and emphasis of the new M3 would have to be different: less visceral, more efficient, more powerful.

Early reports suggested that BMW Motorsport was planning to use a 270bhp version of the 24-valve 2.5-litre six-cylinder engine fitted to the 325i, which would have made the new M3 the first to have a six-cylinder engine. In the event, BMW did use this engine, but decided to stroke it out by 2mm and bore it out slightly to push the capacity up to 2,990cc, so that the eventual power output rose to no less than 286bhp. Evidently, the M3 was to become a true supercar.

By 1992, the environmental lobby in Germany had become sufficiently vocal for BMW to be concerned about the M3. As well as prudently limiting its top speed electronically to 155mph, in line with most other German supercar manufacturers, BMW made efforts to tone down the car's styling. The wide arches of the old M3 would be traded for a very modest tweak in bodywork aerodynamics.

When the advance press pictures were released in June 1992, there was some comment that BMW had perhaps gone too far in the direction of restraint, but in the event BMW was proven to have judged the times correctly.

The first public taste of the M3 came at the October 1992 Paris Salon, when it was displayed alongside the new Motorsport-developed 850CSi. Interestingly, both cars were quoted as having the same 0-62mph times (6.0 seconds) and electronically restricted 155mph top speed.

The bodywork changes were very discreet. Gone were the bulging arches and flagrant rear spoiler of the old M3. At the front there was a new, deep spoiler with a prominent body-colour mesh grille and driving lamps. The side skirts were of a new, chiselled-by-the-wind shape, the rear valance was deeper and incorporated aerodynamic extensions, while the door mirrors had a new aerodynamic profile. Apart from new 10-spoke 17in alloy wheels and a smattering of 'M3' badges, these were the only external messages to tell an M3 from a 325i Coupe.

Of course, the mechanical side of the equation told a different story. The engine was a much modified 3-litre version of the BMW M50 straight-six. It kept the Bosch Motronic DME M3.3 electronic engine management system and VACC (otherwise known as VANOS) variable camshaft timing and, for smoothness, added a new dual-mass flywheel. Twin oxygen sensors and catalysts provided separate fuel/air supply to two sets of three cylinders each.

Total output was 286bhp at 7,000rpm, while maximum torque (236lb.ft) came up at only 3,600rpm; the engine was

Based on the all-new 3 Series Coupe, the 1992 M3 was totally different from the earlier M3 series. It was a much bigger car, more powerful, safer and more rapid. BMW touted it as a Grand Touring car rather than an out-and-out sportscar.

red-lined at a snorting 7,250rpm. The 286bhp power output was identical to that of the M635CSi – surely no coincidence – and BMW claimed that its 96bhp per litre was the best of any normally aspirated road car.

Thanks to the variable cam timing, the torque curve was extraordinary: it remained flat all the way from 3,600 to 5,900rpm: engineers referred to it as 'Ayers Rock'. It also had more torque at idle than the old M3 engine had at maximum kilter! It was also unexpectedly economical, returning an average of 31mpg in the government test cycles. Unlike the old war-painted M3 engines, the new unit had simple crackle black cam covers with plain 'BMW M Power' script.

Performance was a match for the M5 and 835CSi and was much improved over the old M3: BMW claimed 0-62mph in 6.0 seconds and a 155mph top speed (without a restrictor and with different gearing, Motorsport managing director Karl-Heinz Kalbfell suggested the M3 was capable of 175mph). This was despite the fact that the M3 weighed a hefty 1,460kg, some 130kg more than the 325i Coupe.

Some testers managed even better: *Autocar & Motor* magazine scored 0-60mph in 5.4 seconds and even managed to persuade the engine management to cut out at 162 instead of 155mph! In-gear acceleration was also phenomenal and seamlessly delivered, seemingly whatever the gear selected and whatever the speed.

Naturally, the suspension was also tweaked. The general layout of single-joint strut axles at the front and multi-link axles at the rear remained, but the springs became progressive-rate and the dampers were 10 per cent stiffer than the M Technic system fitted to the standard Coupe. Many other suspension components were reinforced: tougher stub-axles and spring plates, thicker anti-roll bars and rear control arms, and rear wheel bearings borrowed from the 8 Series. Modified front track arms altered the geometry. Overall the M3 sat 30mm lower than other 3 Series Coupes.

Additional chassis changes included significantly uprated brakes: over an inch bigger in diameter (inner ventilated front and rear), a larger master-cylinder and revised ABS.

The new M3 was as subtle as the old M3 had been brash. No fat arches and boot spoilers here: instead, BMW designed elegantly chiselled side skirts and rounded door mirrors. Together with a different front bumper/spoiler and five-spoke alloy wheels, these were the only real changes over the standard 3 Series Coupe.

The M3 was very aerodynamic, a fact emphasized by its fluted rear valance. When launched, the M3 cost £32,450, less than the (slower) Porsche 968 and Jaguar XJS.

Underneath the M3, the story was one of increasing sophistication: reinforced suspension, much bigger brakes, speed-sensitive power steering and very wide wheels and tyres.

These 10-spoke wheels were standard equipment on the early E36 M3 coupe, whereas the saloon and convertible each had their own five-spoke variety, all three types of wheel being 17in diameter.

Also new were reworked speed-sensitive power steering, reinforced steering knuckles and wider 235/40 ZR17 tyres (or even fatter rear tyres if you went for the optional 8.5in rear rims).

A limited-slip differential was standard, quite naturally, while the gear ratios were much revised: fifth became direct-drive instead of fourth, as on most other 3 Series models, so that the lower gears could be stacked closer together.

Inside, very little was done to change the cabin. You were provided with new seats in which the upper third and the headrests were adjustable for height to obtain the best shoulder support, while the seat squabs could be extended for optimum thigh support; there was suede-type upholstery for all seat edges. The instruments were now marked in red and, as per Motorsport practice, the fuel economy gauge was replaced by an oil temperature gauge and an 'M' logo was sited in the binnacle and on the gear-knob (which now had a conventional five-speed gate, not the previous dogleg-

first arrangement). You could also opt to delete the standard BMW steering wheel and revert to a leather-trimmed Motorsport wheel with airbag (at a cost of £560).

Other options included air conditioning, metallic paint, wider rear wheels, electrically adjustable front seats, heated front seats, anti-theft system, cruise control, full leather trim and various hi-fi systems. Standard gear included electric windows, central locking and a trip computer.

Testers were struck by how refined and sophisticated the new M3 was, especially when compared with the previous edition. Understandably, some lamented the loss of the old M3's raw spirit, but most donned a pragmatic hat and admitted that this was probably the fastest BMW yet built: while six cylinders certainly robbed the M3 of some of the old guttural roar, it did make it improbably swift and unexpectedly refined. No-one questioned the eager throttle response and seamless quantities of power and torque in all gears.

Equally, the new M3 was bestowed with phenomenal grip and a perfect 50/50 weight distribution. In comparison with the feisty race-inspired feel of the old car, the E36 M3 felt ruthlessly glued in place. Undeniably, it was hugely fast around corners, but perhaps it had lost some of the old M3 magic in the process. BMW itself admitted that the E36 M3 was less a successor to the previous M3 and more a replacement for the M635CSi – a rapid, super-efficient express rather than a raw, on-the-edge, sports coupe.

Initial production was all left-hand drive, and the UK had to wait until August 1993 for the first right-hand-drive cars to come off the line, with a launch price of £32,450 (this was less than the last M3 had cost – and the steering wheel was now in the right place). In total, 270 examples were sold in the UK during 1993, followed by 999 in 1994, the first full year of sales, and 1,409 in 1995.

American customers were able to buy the new M3 from January 1994, but with a much less exotic cylinder head. The net result of this change was a tumble in power output from 286 to 240bhp, although one trade-off was a more flexible torque curve, and by changing the gearing, the US version was very nearly as fast accelerating from rest.

Even before the official launch of the M3, it had been

The M3's interior was every bit as good as that of the 3 Series Coupe on which it was based. First-class ergonomics, space for four adults and excellent equipment levels were strong suits. The sports seats looked great and were very comfortable, although there was some criticism about lack of support.

known that BMW intended to offer the model in Cabriolet and four-door saloon forms. The Cabriolet was the first to arrive (in the spring of 1994), echoing the previous generation of drop-top M3, and on its arrival in the UK it cost some £5,110 more than the Coupe at £38,210.

In broad mechanical terms the Cabriolet was identical to the M3 Coupe, but in its emphasis it was perhaps more effete. There were forged, gloss-polished 7½x17in front and wider 8½x17in rear aluminium wheels. The seats came as standard with nappa leather, and the folding roof (shared with other 3 Series Cabriolet models) was electrically operated; a body-colour hardtop was also on the spec sheet. One further minor change was the deletion of the contoured lip on the deep front spoiler.

Performance was slightly blunted compared with the Coupe because it weighed 1,540kg (some 80kg more than the closed M3) and because its aerodynamics suffered. The 0-62mph acceleration figure was quoted as 6.2 seconds,

while the 50-75mph dash in fourth took 6.9 seconds (half a second slower). Still, no-one could accuse the new car of being slow: indeed, it was one of the quickest four-seater convertibles ever made.

The four-door saloon version of the M3 was perhaps a more surprising development, but again it was perfectly suited to the increasingly sensitive times. It was a method lesson in understatement: no car ever looked so humble yet delivered so much. BMW stated diplomatically: "Driving in a sporting, dynamic style these days means showing genuine fairness and superiority on the road – and this is precisely the philosophy of the M3 saloon."

The engine was exactly the same as in the M3 Coupe and Cabriolet, but there were some softening features. The suspension was retuned for greater comfort, the new five-spoke alloy wheels were M5-inspired (and had wider 8.5in rims at the rear), the front spoiler lip was deleted, the side skirts were toned down, the sports seats were electrically

The M3 family in 1994: saloon, Coupe and Convertible. The saloon and Coupe were identically priced, and the four-door model took almost one in four M3 sales worldwide.

heated and leather-trimmed, the instrument panel and steering wheel were wood-finished, the front doors had storage pockets and the interior door handles were chrome-plated. As with the other M3 variants, a front passenger airbag and exterior temperature gauge were standard. Its price was identical to the Coupe's and BMW (GB) expected a mere 50 to be sold in its first year – 1995.

In performance terms, the 15kg heavier saloon boasted exactly the same figures as the Coupe: 0-62mph in 6.0 seconds and 50-75mph in fourth gear in 6.4 seconds. How many five-seater, four-door cars could claim this sort of crushing speed?

At the opposite end of the scale, an M3 GT was announced by BMW in November 1994, built to comply with 1995 Le Mans regulations. This looked as fierce as the saloon looked mild, with its front airdam splitter and two-tier rear spoiler. Power went up by 9bhp to 295bhp and the suspension was made lower and stiffer. Cosmetically, many interior parts were made from Kevlar, leather trim was

standard, and all GT models were painted the same dark green colour. Weight was all but identical to the standard M3. Only 396 M3 GTs were built, at the equivalent of £2,500 over the usual price, and none came to the UK (officially, at least).

One further special model – for the USA only – was the M3 Lightweight. This was essentially a mildly stripped-out M3 "intended for the serious racer or driving school participant". It made do without a sunroof, insulation, radio or air conditioning, and had aluminium rather than steel doors and a large boot spoiler. Weight dropped by 100kg, enabling BMW to quote a 0-60mph time of 5.8 seconds (0.3 second better than the standard M3). Of course, this might also have been helped by BMW selecting engines off the line which were "at the upper end of design tolerance" – in other words, the best performing engines on the bench were pulled off specially for the Lightweight. Acceleration was also helped by a lower final drive ratio of 3.23:1 (normally 3.15:1). It is believed that only around 85

In late 1995, BMW launched its revised M3 Evolution range. Underneath, that meant a bigger and more powerful engine, a six-speed gearbox and an uprated chassis. Externally, the changes were small: a blacked-out spoiler grille, white indicator lenses and, on the Coupe and Convertible, aluminium doors.

Close-up of the Double VANOS infinitely variable camshaft timing system used in the Evolution engine. Unlike the previous M3 VANOS system, this worked on both the inlet and exhaust valves.

examples of this model were made.

In October 1995, BMW made some very significant changes to the M3, resulting in a car known as the M3 Evolution. The fundamentals of the Evolution were a bigger engine, a six-speed gearbox and chassis revisions, the most significant of these being the new engine. It was developed over a three-year period by the same team as were responsible for the McLaren F1 V12, and it was widely quoted that the new engine was effectively "half of a McLaren F1 engine", since the internal dimensions of the V12 engine were almost shared with the previous BMW 'six'. That may have been stretching the point, but the new engine certainly featured some impressive new engineering.

By raising the bore slightly (86.4 against 86.0mm) and lengthening the stroke (up by 4.2mm to 91.0mm), capacity was now 3,201cc and the compression ratio was raised to 11.3:1. Other changes included lightweight pistons, an improved two-mass flywheel, a modified vibration damper, low-friction graphite-coated conrods, larger-diameter inlet

The extra power of the 3.2-litre engine made the M3 range even quicker. The 0-60mph acceleration time was now less than 5.5 seconds, but an equally impressive statistic was braking to rest from 100kmh (62mph), which took only 2.8 seconds, thanks to one of the most sophisticated anti-lock braking systems in the world.

valves, a second oil pump to offset the effect of greater cornering forces, a revised exhaust manifold and two quick-start metal catalysts.

In an effort to reduce emissions and noise and improve fuel consumption, BMW developed its own new MSS50 digital electronic management system – the first instance of a car manufacturer creating an in-house engine management system. It was a collaboration between electronics experts at BMW and at Siemens and was said to be capable of issuing 20 million instructions per second. Its function was to provide cylinder specific injection, all ignition functions (solid-state electronic with six individual coils), anti-knock controls (because BMW said any grade of unleaded fuel could be used) and full electronic engine mapping for the revised VANOS infinitely variable camshaft timing for both inlet and exhaust valves (the previous system worked only on the inlet camshaft – this was why the new system was dubbed Double VANOS). There was also more: the clever black box monitored engine oil levels and the fuel cut-off for the immobilizer, it ran a catalyst protection programme, an engine overrun control and was fully self-diagnostic. It's not surprising that BMW claimed this was the most advanced management system ever applied to a road car.

The new MSS50 system was the key to the Evolution's amazing efficiency. The new engine offered a 9 per cent increase in torque to 258lb.ft at a low 3,250rpm. Power went up by an even greater margin, to 321bhp at 7,400rpm – putting it over the magic 100bhp-per-litre mark, and offering the highest specific output of any BMW road car engine except the V12 in the McLaren F1. At the same time, fuel consumption as measured by government norms improved by 6.2 per cent over the previous M3 (up to an amazing 32.3mpg).

That was how BMW managed to improve performance and more than satisfy toughening emissions regulations for its high-performance engine. There were also tough new standards on noise pollution to consider; along with the obvious marketing benefits, this was the main reason why BMW chose a six-speed gearbox. It was derived from the M5 gearbox, with ratios suitably altered for the M3; sixth gear was now an overdrive, which significantly helped fuel

The Evolution interior remained little changed. This is the cabin of the Convertible, with its standard leather upholstery and comfort-orientated BMW sports seats.

consumption, while the bottom three ratios were made shorter and fourth became slighty taller. Interestingly, the top speed of 155mph could be reached in fifth gear as well as sixth, and even in fourth you could reach 138mph. BMW engineers reckoned that, if you removed the restrictor, no less than 180mph would be a realistic maximum.

Underneath the M3, more changes were wrought. Dampers and springs were all-new and the steering was revised to give more feel (it had a marginally quicker rack without speed-sensitive weighting). The front brakes now came from the M5, those racing-derived 'floating' two-part discs which are fully described in Chapter 7; the M5 also donated its 25 per cent limited-slip differential. In the braking department, better heat dissipation and a longer service life were claimed (M3 brakes were inevitably heavily abused). An all-new ABS system was fitted: the Teves MkIV, specially developed for the Evolution. BMW claimed

that the new M3 could screech to a halt from 62mph in just 2.8 seconds.

Since the new car took only 5.5 seconds to reach 62mph from rest, it should be plain that the Evolution had stepped up a league in performance terms. BMW now claimed a 50-75mph acceleration time in fourth gear of just 5.7 seconds (the old M3 took 6.4 seconds). Top speed remained limited electronically to 155mph.

External changes were almost non-existent. The indicator lenses were now clear, there was a new high-level third brake light and the grille was matt black instead of colour-coded to the rest of the body. Less obvious was the choice of aluminium for the doors (on the Coupe and Cabriolet only), saving 12kg each side. Three new colours were added: Estoril Blue, Techno Violet and Byzantium.

Inside there was a new fabric for the seats called M-Cross, with the usual Amaretta edging. Full leather remained an option, in five colours, including Modena Nature for the first time. One final change was an automatically dimming interior mirror.

Intially only the Coupe body was produced, but by early 1996, all three body styles were on offer for the Evolution, and a number of differences persisted between them. All three had unique wheel designs: the Coupe had natty 10-spoked M-Style Double Spoke II alloys, the Cabriolet had M-Style Double Spoke five-spokers and the saloon was equipped with M-Contour II five-spokers. All were now shod with 225/45 R17 rubber at the front and 245/40 R17 at the back (ie, narrower front and wider rear tyres).

The Coupe made do with a spacesaver spare wheel to free up more room in the boot. Main specification differences over the other two M3 models were integrated headrests in the M Sports seats, M-tuned sports suspension and a 'through-load facility'.

The Cabriolet, of course, still had its electric soft-top, electric rear windows and automatic roll-over protection system. It made do with less exotic BMW sports seats, but added such items as M-tuned sports suspension, a rear armrest, leather upholstery and metallic paint.

The saloon also had ordinary BMW sports seats, electric rear windows, a rear centre armrest and leather upholstery,

The M3 saloon persisted as a popular member of the Evolution line-up. A host of minor differences confirmed its role as the discreet performer of the M3 family.

but in addition it boasted burr walnut for the centre console, door pulls and gear-knob and a front centre armrest. However, it did not have M-tuned suspension, merely BMW sports suspension.

German prices were the equivalent of £1,600 higher than before when sales began in late 1995. The UK waited until all Evolution models were available, sales beginning in February 1996, when prices were rather higher than for the old M3: £36,550 for the Coupe and saloon, £41,800 for the Cabriolet.

Testers were enthralled by the new M3, the extra power catapulting the model into unassailable performance territory. While the experience was more refined and quieter than in the previous M3, it was still a thunderous experience. Likewise, the revised suspension geometry (notably increased castor) improved stability and reduced oversteer: it was now near-impossible to boot the rear end out of line in the dry. Less exciting, perhaps, but that was what BMW thought its customers wanted.

Despite the Evolution's emissions and noise-conscious changes, American customers were presented with a rather different M3. The engine had a slightly shorter stroke (89.6 versus 91.0mm), so its capacity was lower at 3,152cc, while the compression ratio remained at 10.5:1. Output was a

comparatively disappointing 243bhp SAE at 6,000rpm and torque was also down at 236lb.ft at 3,800rpm. One last ignominy was the retention of a five-speed gearbox.

A further evolution of the M3 was an optional sequential gearbox, first seen in July 1996 and available on left-hand-drive cars from the autumn of that year. Sequential M Gearbox (SMG), as it was called, featured a computerized, hydraulically controlled clutch, which did away with the need for a clutch pedal and worked with a six-speed manual-based gearbox (ie, unlike most sequential systems, this one was not based on an automatic transmission burdened with power-quelling torque converters).

The sequential system allowed for two programmes: fully automatic E (Economy) mode or manual S (Sports) mode. These were arranged in two planes: E on the right-hand side and S on the left, with simple plus and minus signs to indicate up or down changes, all operated by a stubby aluminium-and-leather gear-knob. In S mode, gearchanges were instantaneous – you did not need to lift your foot from the accelerator. After heavy braking, the gearbox even selected the correct gear for you automatically. A small light under the 'M' logo in the dash lit up when the rev-limit was reached.

At an equivalent of £2,500, this was an expensive option, and many questioned the value of a system which was a

First available in 1996, the Sequential M Gearbox (SMG) was an interesting option, allowing Touring Car-style gearchanges via an 'up-or-down' gear lever. When canted over to the right, the lever performed in Economy mode (fully automatic), but if you pushed it over to the left, it transferred to manual Sports mode.

compromise: slower to change than a manual gearbox, yet not as smooth as a true automatic. In truth, despite its Touring Car racing connotations, it was a system designed for convenience more than pleasure; after all, the M3 was not available with automatic transmission.

In the UK, a semi-M model called the 328i Sport was launched in September 1995, shortly before the new right-hand-drive Evolution was introduced. This had an M body kit and M-tuned suspension and showed how far the M philosophy had filtered down to other models in the BMW range.

When you opted for the SMG system, a display was included in the rev-counter indicating whether you were in Sports or Economy mode, and which gear had been selected. When the rev-limit was reached, a Touring Car-style light flashed up under the 'M' logo to indicate that an up-change was required. This driver is being asked to change up to sixth at 250kmh/155mph!

The 1997 model year M3s (available from September 1996) shared the subtle new grille design of all 3 Series models. The BMW kidney grille became more rounded, with chunkier brightwork, and a new panel surrounded the headlamps. Other changes included seat belt pretensioners, a IIIG EWS remote alarm and a new design of M Sport steering wheel incorporating an airbag.

The trio of M3 Evolution models remain available at the time of writing. Worldwide sales of the M3 were the best of any M car ever: 6,712 in 1993, 10,764 in 1994, 11,964 in 1995 and 11,789 in 1996. Such figures enabled BMW to claim that the M3 was taking over 50 per cent of sales in the high-performance sector – an extraordinary success which confirmed that BMW had got its planning exactly right.

In 1996, details leaked out of tentative plans to offer an M3 Compact model based on the truncated-tail base 3 Series model. It was to have the 321bhp Evolution engine and modified M Roadster rear suspension, and *Auto Motor und Sport* magazine in Germany even built their own interpretation of the M3 Compact ideal. It seemed at the time of writing, however, that such a car would not actually reach the public since the all-new 3 Series was due for launch in spring 1998. An M3 version of that model, though, looked a near-certainty.

CHAPTER 5

The first M535i (E12)

An affordable 5 Series M car – 1979-81

With the letter M firmly established in the car world's consciousness through the immense publicity gained by the M1, BMW set about bringing its Motorsport marque to the common man. The car chosen to do this was the E12 5 Series.

It is a little known fact that, during the 1970s, BMW Motorsport created a number of special one-off cars for important customers and senior management personnel, usually based on the current 5 Series. In BMW's own words: "These were very special 5 Series saloons hand-built with painstaking care and featuring the largest possible six-cylinder power units taken from BMW's wide range of engines (sometimes specially tuned for higher performance). The engineers at BMW Motorsport GmbH also took a close look at the chassis and brakes of these cars." One well-known such car was the 1974 3-litre CSL-engined 5 Series built for BMW GB's managing director, Jonathan Sieff.

In a retrospective review, BMW said of these cars: "They did their own advertising and won over more and more enthusiasts, literally shaking up the sports car world at the time. BMW M cars soon became very well known, even though production remained limited to an ultra-small series of models built exclusively to order."

On a more commercial note, in 1978 BMW briefly offered a catalogued 3.3-litre Motorsport conversion for two models in the E12 5 Series line-up: the 525 and 528i could be transformed with a 197bhp 633CSi engine, close-ratio gearbox, limited-slip diff and wide BBS 7x14in alloy wheels with Motorsport centres. Although an unofficial model, this was a definite precursor to the M535i and the first real public offering from BMW Motorsport GmbH.

However, it was the 1979 M535i which really brought the 'M' prefix into the public domain. Potential buyers first saw the new M535i at the September 1979 Frankfurt show. BMW stated: "The M535i represents a perfect symbiosis: First, it bears the name of a demanding manufacturer of standard production automobiles – a manufacturer which guarantees optimum production quality and a perfect finish. Second, it is the special product of a team of motor racing experts – a team that is able to combine its dedication and motor racing involvement with industrial resources, scientific know-how, and professional efficiency."

The M535i's trump card was that it used essentially the same M49 engine as the M1, albeit in a milder state of tune – in fact it was identical to the contemporary 635CSi. That meant six cylinders, 3.5 litres, Bosch L-Jetronic injection and a very healthy 218bhp at 5,200rpm and 224lb.ft of torque at 4,000rpm.

The Getrag five-speed gearbox was the same close-ratio unit as fitted to some 528i models, where fifth represented direct drive and first gear was canted over to the left, dog-leg style. However, the final drive was 'taller' than on any other model in the 5 Series line-up: there was a choice of 3.25 or 3.07:1 (compared with 3.45:1 for the 528i). It seemed only natural that no automatic transmission should be offered. Uprated ventilated front and solid rear disc brakes fitted with four-piston calipers brought the M535i up

The soul of discretion: the M535i was almost slavishly similar to the rest of the 5 Series range, which was certainly a major component in its roster of attractions. Its only distinguishing features were the deep front spoiler and wider wheels and tyres.

The 3.5-litre engine of the M535i was taken directly from the 635CSi Coupe. That meant it lacked the BMW Motorsport stamping of most other M cars, but at least its 218bhp was effortlessly and reliably delivered. The level of torque available was even more impressive.

On the move, the M535i was extremely swift – indeed, faster than the 635CSi with which it shared its engine. BMW quoted a top speed of 138mph and 0-100kmh (0-62mph) in 7.5 seconds. Few other cars of the day – whether saloons or sportscars – could match this sort of performance, let alone seat five adults in comfort.

square in no uncertain terms. Although the suspension was kept largely the same, the Bilstein dampers were specially valved for the M car.

For its day, this was a very rapid saloon car. Indeed, it was BMW's fastest machine if you excluded the M1. BMW claimed a top speed of 138mph (222kmh) and a 0-100kmh sprint of 7.5 seconds. This was even faster than the 635CSi from which the M car took its engine, but then, at 1,465kg, it was marginally lighter.

The M535i's light-alloy wheels were wider than those of other six-cylinder 5 Series models (6.5x14in) while the tyres (Michelin XRX) remained the same 195/70 VR14 size as for the 528i. Otherwise it was very difficult to tell an M535i

apart from any other member of the 5 Series range unless you opted for the no-cost option of aerodynamic aids: a deep front airdam/body-coloured bumper and a black rubber rear spoiler, plus optional Motorsport stripes in the traditional colour scheme.

Inside, four Recaro seats were standard, as well as a leather-trimmed sports steering wheel borrowed from the M1. BMW made no attempt to make the M535i a lightweight, preferring to keep such luxury items as a sunroof, central locking and electrically adjustable mirrors.

Production of the M535i began in April 1980, priced at DM35,100 in Germany. The model reached the UK in right-hand-drive form in September 1980 with a price tag of

Luxury and sportiness graced the M535i interior. While it lacked the 'M' branding of later M series cars, it still felt special thanks to the M1 steering wheel and Recaro seats.

Because this original-shape (E12) M535i was eventually replaced by the much more boxy-style E28 version, some people are still confused as to which model came first. The clue is to check the width of the kidney-shaped grille, which on BMWs have generally tended to grow wider with each model change.

The rear spoiler was an optional extra, and although intended to perform an aerodynamic function, it also provided a most convenient mounting for the car's badging.

The 14in BBS cross-spoke alloy wheels on the M535i have 6.5in rims and should carry 195/70 VR-rated tyres.

£13,745, over £3,000 more than the 528i, but considerably less than any 6 Series BMW or the similarly-engined 735i saloon.

It was well received in the press as the king of Q cars with an impressively wide range of talents. As Georg Kacher asked in *Car* magazine: "Does this Motor Sport *wunderwagen* have no faults at all?" Apart from some wind noise, inadequate ventilation and braking in the wet, the answer was "No". "The M535i is a car of a piece. Its greatest asset is its overall balance."

The M535i was withdrawn in May 1981 with no direct replacement after a total of only 1,410 cars had been made. Only around 450 were right-hand drive, and of these 408 came to the UK. However, a further 240 CKD (complete knocked down) kits were despatched abroad, including BMW South Africa, where the local assembly plant in Rosslyn built and offered the M535i in its home market. One interesting footnote is that, purely as an experiment, BMW Motorsport fitted a full-house 277bhp M1-spec engine into an E12 5 Series. That car never made it to the market, but it clearly anticipated what would happen with the first M5 some years later.

CHAPTER 6

The E28 twins – M535i and M5

Two stages of Q-car evolution – 1984-88

Invariably with BMW M products, there will be a gap between the launch of a new BMW mainstream model and the arrival of its Motorsport-tweaked version. Often this will be a long time (witness the seven years it took for an M version of the 6 Series to appear), and the new E28 5 Series of 1981 was no exception.

This boxy new-generation 5 Series represented a very conservative evolution of the old shape. The top model in the launch line-up was the 184bhp six-cylinder 528i, but there was always a desire to instal something even more tractable in the 5 Series. In March 1982, BMW replaced the old M1-type twin-cam 3,453cc engine in the 635CSi with a new 3,430cc single-overhead-camshaft unit developing 218bhp, and this was an obvious choice for fitment into the E28.

Thus, at the October 1984 Paris Salon, BMW announced the latest BMW M car, the M535i. In fact this was one of a pair of 3.5-litre 5 Series cars, since a lesser sister model also became available, simply called the 535i. Mechanically, the two models were identical – the only instance of an M car not having an uprated engine compared with a production model. Many observers opined that therefore the M535i was not a true M car. Certainly, its specification was not as exciting, nor as special, as other Motorsport-developed cars, but this ignores the fact that, by 1984, BMW Motorsport GmbH had already identified a growing market which its products could exploit.

In BMW's own words: "The M symbol can now be used to express what a number of very different products have in common: Grand Prix engines and a collection of sportswear fashions, high-performance, top-of-the-range vehicles in the individual BMW series and one-off sports jobs built by BMW Motorsport GmbH, such as the M1... There is thus more behind 'M' than just a particular technical concept, more than just a mere product designation. It unites under a common banner a range of rather special products."

The M535i was less a product of M Power (the engine tuning and manufacturing wing) and far more a product of M Technics, the branch which was responsible for 'equipment of particular technical sophistication'. Nothing was done to the 635CSi engine, but instead, virtually everything that made the M535i special was cosmetic, which is why many enthusiasts react with horror at the mention of the E28 M535i in the same breath as other M cars.

Indeed, the only technical changes required for the installation of the 3.5-litre engine were highly marginal. The 528i donated, in completely standard form, its five-speed ZF gearbox, variable-weight power-assisted recirculating-ball steering and ABS-equipped all-round disc brakes (ventilated at the front), but the M535i did gain mildly uprated springs and Bilstein gas dampers at both ends, plus thicker anti-roll bars. A 25 per cent limited-slip differential was standard. Options included a switchable four-speed automatic gearbox (yet more ammunition for those who were suspicious of the M535i), a five-speed Getrag close-ratio gearbox with dogleg first gear (to redeem it slightly), air conditioning and cruise control.

The E28 M535i was quite the inverse of the previous incarnation: all show, but no extra go. For this reason, it is rightly regarded as a lesser species of M fish, and is often completely discounted as a 'real' M car. Special wheels and body-coloured skirts and spoilers barked louder than the car could bite.

The 3.4-litre single-overhead-camshaft engine was the next generation of BMW 'six', coming from the current 635CSi and developing 218bhp (identical to the last M535i). Note the absence of any Motorsport lettering, since the M division had no input in this department.

Bodywork changes were more far-reaching. To offset the fitment of wider alloy wheels (165x390mm) and tyres (220/55 VR390), some aerodynamic modifications were made: the front airdam was deeper, the sills were broader, the rear valance was extended downwards and the bootlid was topped off with a spoiler. BMW claimed that the M535i shared its drag coefficient of 0.37 with the base-model 518i. 'M' badges on the grille and boot identified the Motorsport connection.

Inside, there were also a few changes. The front seats were similar to those of the M635CSi, with adjustable thigh supports, and the steering wheel was a Sport item, coloured in Motorsport livery on one spoke (which also recurred on the seats). Standard equipment included a trip computer, electric windows and heated electric door mirrors.

The M535i was launched in Britain – alongside the standard 535i – in January 1985. The cost was £17,950, which was around £2,000 more than the top-spec 528i SE. For the extra performance, the premium was more than justified: BMW claimed a top speed of 143mph and *Autocar*

magazine tested one from 0-60mph in 7.4 seconds, some 1.3 seconds quicker than the 528i. Whether the M Technic kit was worth the extra £800 over the more sober 535i is a different question, but history will always regard the M535i benignly: after all, it does have 'the most powerful letter in the world' on it. And in truth, it was a great driver's car for its day.

A catalyzed M535i was sold in certain markets with an emasculated 185bhp engine, which gave it a performance more in keeping with the 528i (about 133mph top speed), which seemed rather pointless. The United States had to make do with the 535iS, a bespoilered 535i with lower suspension.

M5 – The real 'M' 5 Series

Considering the direction the M535i had taken – basically appealing to a new marketing-invented creature called the yuppie – it must have been a relief to engineers and enthusiasts alike when BMW set out to do a 'proper' Motorsport 5 Series: the M5. In comparison with the

Many observers felt that the 'M' symbol (described by BMW as 'the most powerful letter in the world') had been somehow diluted by adorning the M535i.

Rear spoiler, deep rear bumper valance and badging singled the M535i out over its near-identical sister, the standard 535i.

M535i, the modifications were pointedly antithetical: cosmetically, the M5 would be stripped of its bodykit, and instead, everything of importance happened underneath that sober-looking body.

The heart of the new M5 was the familiar twin-cam 3,453cc engine, as fitted to the M635CSi and developing 286bhp. It had to be inclined at 30 degrees to fit under the bonnet (with as little as an inch of clearance). This crackle-black and aluminium-topped powerplant looked as purposeful in the 5 Series engine bay as it ever had in the M1.

BMW Motorsport also went much further with the rest of the mechanical specification. The sports-tuned suspension featured shorter progressive-rate springs and single-tube Bilstein gas dampers, as on the M535i, and there was patented Track-link rear suspension. New were reinforced disc brakes with extra-large calipers, high-geared steering, a

In line with its cosmetic approach, the 5 Series dash remained pretty standard: no 'M' logos or oil pressure gauges here. The sports steering wheel had Motorsport stripes on the lower spoke.

Despite the lukewarm specification compared with other M cars, the M535i was a fast machine in absolute terms: BMW claimed 145mph and 0-60mph in 7.0 seconds. However, the rear subframe layout caused handling problems in the wet and could engender uncomfortable vibration.

Back to the future: BMW returned to its *modus operandi* of discretion in valour with the genuine M5. It had a similar style of front spoiler to its M535i cousin and even wider alloy wheels and tyres, but otherwise it looked essentially the same as any other 5 Series. However, each example was painstakingly hand-built by BMW Motorsport.

When the M5 driver put his foot down, the car simply took off. BMW claimed a top speed of 153mph and 0-60mph in 6.2 seconds, all to the gruff sound of the twin exhaust pipes. Handling was much better than with other 5 Series cars, thanks to the Motorsport team's attention.

specially designed ABS system and a reinforced version of the Getrag 280/5 five-speed gearbox as also fitted to the M635CSi (with a standard shift pattern). Weight distribution was helped by relocating the beefier 90amp-hour battery to the velour-carpeted boot.

The M5's exterior was only extreme in the level of its understatement: wide BBS spoked alloy wheels and 225/55 VR tyres, a subtly deepened front spoiler, the most discreet 'M5' badging front and rear, and body-coloured door mirrors – that was all. As well as the standard paint colours, the M5 could be ordered in salmon-silver metallic at extra cost. Later examples also had a boot-mounted black spoiler, but the Cd was a brick-like 0.38 – which went to show just how effective were the M535i's spoilers, disliked though they were by many.

The changes inside were equally modest. There were velour quality carpets for the floors, doors and parcel shelf, Highland fabric for the door inserts and seats, an 'M' logo on the rev-counter, 'M5' badges on the sill kick-plates, electrically adjustable BMW sports seats and a leather-

M Power says it all: here was the 286bhp M635CSi engine looking very much at home, despite the pronounced angle at which it had to be installed. Since the M5 weighed 1,470kg – less than the M635CSi – this was comfortably the quickest car made by BMW in 1985.

The M5's leather Motorsport steering wheel dominates the cabin. Other clues that this is a special M car include the 'M' logo in the rev-counter, 'M5' logos on the door sill plates, and electrically adjustable sports seats.

bound M Sports steering wheel with Motorsport colours around one of its three spokes, on the seats and on the gear-knob.

There really was very little to tell this super high-performance machine apart from other four-door 5 Series saloons. Yet this innocuous looking projectile was capable of an astonishing 153mph, could reach 60mph from rest in 6.2 seconds and do the 50-75mph sprint in direct fourth gear in 7.7 seconds. Testers eulogized this 'Q-car among Q-cars'. *Car* magazine recorded the fastest time for any four-door saloon car around Castle Combe racing circuit (close to 90mph average) and was rightly impressed: "A very superior sports saloon," it said.

The suspension tweaks seemed to have cured to a large degree the E28 5 Series' Achilles' heel, namely the oversteer and vibration engendered by its rear subframe layout. Care was still required in the wet, but in the dry, grip was much better and the handling was enjoyably correctable.

The M5 was actually in existence before the public knew about it. The first batch of production (which began in October 1984) was exclusively for special, favoured customers. The M5's first public showing did not come until the February 1985 Amsterdam motor show, one

Two views of the purposeful M5, which was always a rare sight in Britain, perhaps because it cost half as much again as the M535i. Well over half of all M5 production went to the USA.

month before its planned debut at Geneva, simply because the catalyzed version of the engine was not ready and BMW did not want to be accused of eco-insensitivity in the Swiss market. The cost in Germany was DM80,750 (over DM30,000 more than the M535i).

At first, BMW wanted production not to exceed 250 units per year. In fact, the numbers built were significantly higher than this, mainly because of a late rush of American production (and these US cars were not bespoke-built). European cars were hand-built to special order only by a 75-strong team on a BMW Motorsport production line: painted and prepared bodyshells would be delivered from the main line at Dingolfing and married to engines and suspensions at Preussenstrasse, the whole process taking a week to complete. This arrangement also meant you could tailor your car with, for example, buffalo hide trim, electric rear seats and any colour scheme you wanted; BMW invited customers to come and see their car being built, a tradition it would continue with subsequent M5 models.

Britain had to wait for a right-hand-drive M5 to be

This late UK-registered M5 has different alloy wheels, largely blacked-out brightwork and a black boot spoiler. It was not unknown for M5 owners to fit M535i-type body kits, which lost some of the subtlety of the original, but announced that you were driving something a bit special.

specially engineered, including such details as a resited master-cylinder to improve brake feel. The UK-spec M5 finally arrived in July 1986. At £31,295, it was over 50 per cent more costly than the M535i, but justified it by having many additional items of standard equipment, including air conditioning, metallic paint and an electric sunroof. A total of 177 right-hand-drive cars were imported to the UK. Apart from CKD units, production finished at the end of 1987.

American buyers received the M5 even later, in February 1987 as a 1988 model year car. This version had larger front and rear bumpers, side reflectors and a fixed specification: black paint, blacked-out brightwork and tan leather upholstery. It also made do with an emissions-restricted 256bhp, making it notably slower than the European M5. It was announced that America would receive only a limited run of 500 M5s, but when the eventual run reached 1,235 cars, due to unprecedented demand, some owners got together to file a lawsuit claiming false advertising. BMW's response was a settlement consisting of a credit note towards the purchase of a new BMW for every M5 buyer .

Total production of the M5 had reached 2,145 by the end of production in December 1987, plus a further 96 cars supplied in CKD form for assembly abroad (CKD production actually continued until June 1988). To that total could be added a further 9,483 examples of the lesser M535i – at that stage, the best-selling car to wear the coveted 'M' badge.

CHAPTER 7

The delectable M5 (E34)

Masterpiece of understatement – 1988-95

In January 1988, BMW launched perhaps the most effective saloon car the world had ever seen when the new E34 5 Series replaced the old model. BMW Motorsport was especially keen to work its magic on this new car, and it brought the new M5 to production in record time. The new model made its debut in September 1988, and like its predecessor was every inch the understated express.

The engine remained the faithful M1-derived 24-valve six-cylinder unit, but it was extensively revised for its new home. It needed a catalytic converter to meet US emissions standards, but engineers insisted that nevertheless the engine should be even more powerful and boast more torque. Some fairly radical changes ensured that it succeeded on both scores..

The main change was an increase in capacity to 3,535cc, achieved by stretching the stroke by 2mm and resulting in the largest six-cylinder engine BMW had yet produced. This was only the start, however. The valves were now operated by twin cams with a higher lift and different timing, the compression ratio was now 10:1, the crankshaft became a forged and twisted item with 12 counterbalance weights, there was a new flywheel, and platinum hot-wire air mass induction metering from the 750i was installed.

Another very clever device was the competition-inspired electronic butterfly valve in the inlet manifold. The M5 was the first BMW to gain this feature, which made use of natural resonance within the manifold to create a charge effect. Between 2,500 and 4,250rpm, and between 6,750 and the upper rev-limit of 7,200rpm, the valve would close, effectively achieving variable-length intake pipes and boosting torque in those rev-bands. BMW also claimed that throttle response was greatly improved, thanks to this manifold resonance and the use of six separate throttles. Some testers said it was perhaps a little too keen, to the point of being jerky.

To be clean, the exhaust gases were treated by a Lambda-controlled three-way catalyzer. There was even a secondary fan system to pump air into the exhaust manifold when starting from cold, so that emissions could be reduced while the catalyst warmed up.

Overall output was an impressive 315bhp, a rise of 29bhp over the still-current 3,453cc M635CSi engine, while 266lb.ft of torque also made this an enthusiastic puller, especially as 80 per cent of this figure was available from 2,500rpm (thanks to the butterfly-valved manifold). BMW said with some justification that this was "the most powerful production saloon in the world".

Quoted performance was equally impressive: 0-62mph in 6.3 seconds is fast for a sportscar, let alone a hefty four-door luxury saloon. BMW limited the M5's top speed electronically to 155mph, a fop to environmentalists and "as a contribution toward quietening down discussion on possible road traffic limitations".

The chassis was also significantly uprated. In comparison with the standard 535i, suspension was lowered by 20mm and a self-levelling rear axle kept the rear wheels in line whatever the load. Both anti-roll bars were thicker, up from

23 to 25mm at the front and from 15 to 18mm at the rear. The springs were 25 per cent stiffer and the twin-tube gas dampers were tuned to match.

The suspension incorporated what BMW referred to as 'elasto-kinematics'. That meant that the bushes for the rear wheels were compliant in such a way as to permit the whole axle to toe-in under cornering, generating understeer. As drivers of older BMWs will confirm, a degree of understeer is a welcome change from the tail-happy antics of certain 3 and 5 Series models, especially in wet conditions.

The distinctive new patented alloy wheels were extremely clever. Although they looked like steel discs, what you saw was only a pressure-cast magnesium alloy cover. Underneath lay two-piece five-spoke 8x17in alloy wheels; the magnesium alloy turbine covers, with their two concentric sets of blades, sucked 25 per cent more air onto the brake discs as the wheels revolved (the patterns were different on the left and right sides). Engineers claimed the

The heart of the M5 remained essentially the faithful M1-type 'six', but it was stroked out to 3,535cc and produced no less than 315bhp. This made it the largest 'six' BMW had ever made and was the most powerful engine in its range.

Deconstructed M5 engine bares its cutting-edge technology: electronic butterfly inlet valving, hot-wire induction metering, three-way catalysation with a secondary fan to cut emissions during warm-up and six separate throttles.

time taken to cool the brake discs from 400 to 200°C was thereby reduced by 11 per cent.

The front brakes, too, were uprated. The ventilated front discs – already the largest in their class on the 5 Series – grew from 302 to 315mm diameter, while thickness increased by 5mm to 28mm. Also, the fuel tank was expanded from 80 to 90 litres.

Tyres were specified after extensive testing at the Nürburgring, and BMW favoured Pirelli P700 or Michelin 235/45 ZR17 rubber. Interestingly, the wheels had a cast ridge around their rims (which BMW curiously called an "asymmetric hump system"!). This held the tyre in place if it deflated, effectively bringing about a run-flat system.

The power steering was now weighted according to engine speed rather than road speed, and was designed to give more feel and more direct action (the ratio dropped to 15.6:1 from 16.8:1).

Like the previous M5, the 1988 version featured unique

preloaded gear wheels in the five-speed gearbox, but the system was improved, giving even greater selection smoothness and quieter functioning. The ratios of the first three gears were stacked closer together than on the 535i, but the final drive was not as tall (3.91:1, compared with the 535i's 3.45:1).

The aerodynamic changes were so subtle as to be almost invisible. The small front spoiler, rear apron and side skirts were painted a dark colour so that you hardly noticed them, but they had a marked effect. Despite its fatter tyres and larger front cooling inlets, the M5 had an identical drag coefficient to the 535i of 0.32. BMW also made play of the fact that, compared with the previous M5, lift was reduced by 54 per cent at the front and 20 per cent at the rear, and was now identical on both axles. That balance took full advantage of the M5's inherently perfect 50/50 weight distribution.

Other distinguishing features were hard to spot: a black plastic panel between the rear lights, 70mm polished twin exhaust tailpipes, two extra ducts in the front spoiler to cool the radiator and oil cooler, 'M5' badging and, of course, the newly developed M Technic light-alloy wheels. A rear spoiler became a no-cost option from November 1988, and you could choose to delete all the brightwork at extra cost.

Paint choice was mainly metallic: Diamond Black, Salmon Silver, Royal Blue and Malachite Green came from the existing 5 Series range, but Macao Blue and Sebring Grey were exclusive to the M5, as was non-metallic Misano Red (Alpine White and Black were also offered). Aerodynamic parts were contrasted in Sebring Grey metallic or Diamond Black metallic.

Inside you could choose between new silver M Style check fabric or the optional full nappa or buffalo hide in a variety of colours (covering the seats, roof lining and even, on request, the boot). The leather-edged seats were almost infinitely adjustable (optionally electronic), and the individual rear seats were separated by a fixed central armrest incorporating the unusual feature of an extending drawer, in addition to a locker between the rear seats. Head restraints were standard at the back (optionally they would retract automatically when the seat belts were fastened).

From September 1990, the individual rear seats and fixed armrest became optional. The boot was trimmed in velour instead of wool and storage boxes were provided on both sides, plus a retaining net.

The steering wheel was a unique three-spoke leather-covered design with moulded-in thumb grips and the inevitable 'M' logo. The dials were given red needles and the speedo was recalibrated to 300kmh (186mph), and the rev-counter was red-lined between 7,200 and 8000rpm. As with the M3, the econometer in the base of the rev-counter was replaced by an oil temperature gauge and an 'M' symbol appeared between the two major dials. Other interior details included an illuminated M Technic gear-knob, M Technic footrest, colour-coded seat belts and computer-controlled ventilation.

The standard equipment list was lengthy indeed, including ABS, electric windows, PAS, on-board computer, LSD, electric sunroof, air conditioning, headlamp wash and a 750i-derived 'active check control' warning panel to advise of an overload on the self-levelling rear suspension, an open door or bootlid, and lights on or failed. All this extra electrical equipment meant uprating the battery to 85amps and the alternator to 115amps.

Since the M5 was hand-built, BMW took full advantage of its flexibility on options. Special-equipment extras included a car 'phone, electrically adjustable driver's seat with position memory, adjustable rear seat position, body-colour rear spoiler (at no extra cost), de-chroming, 12-channel hi-fi speaker system and even wider rear wheels and tyres (9x17in with 255/40 ZR17 tyres). As far as trim and paint were concerned, your M5 could be tailor-finished by BMW M GmbH to any specification.

The M5 was deliberately marketed as an understated machine. BMW thought its main appeal would be to luxury sportscar drivers needing more space (Porsche and Ferrari were singled out in internal communications), drivers of exclusive makes like Jaguar and Mercedes-Benz, and of tuned cars such as Alpina and Brabus. As BMW put it, "the M5 is a high performance sportscar with the character of a saloon". BMW saw the Ferrari-engined Lancia Thema 8.32 as one major competitor, but highlighted its front-wheel

Thundering performance which no driver of a four-door saloon could ever presume to ask for was the M5's birthright. It could reach 60mph in a fraction over 6 seconds and pulled effortlessly to a restricted top speed of 155mph. Compliant rear suspension helped the M5 become a safe yet enjoyable driver's car.

Ingenious new wheels were a BMW patent. They looked modest enough, but that was down to the magnesium covers. Underneath lay five-spoke alloy wheels fitted with vaned extra rims which delivered 25 per cent more cooling air to the brakes. It was said that, in some cases, this feature alone was sufficient to sell M5s to customers.

drive, smaller size and dull appearance as demerits. It also admitted that the four-door Maserati 430 accelerated faster than the M5, but that its smaller size relegated it to a class below.

BMW even asked Niki Lauda to give an independent report on the new M5. In it he commented: "I regard the M5 as a sportscar shaped like a saloon which is suitable for unrestricted everyday use... You can experience practically all the driving sensations that are possible in a car. The engine is happy at high speeds so you can drive fast on motorways or, thanks to the high torque even at low engine speeds, trundle along in traffic, all without inflicting damage on the engine. No matter what the situation, you always feel there is more power available, and that is very pleasing.

"From the point of view of road characteristics and handling, I think the M5 is quite simply perfect... The brakes are also outstanding... All in all, I believe the M5 is the best M package that BMW has ever produced." Lauda's involvement anticipated many other racing drivers' selection of the M5 as their personal transport.

The M5 was different to the M3 in one major respect: it was hand-built at Garching by BMW Motorsport. Bodyshells would be delivered from the main line in Dingolfing, ready for two employees to build up each car, taking six weeks to finish; only 100 of BMW M's 450-strong staff were actually involved in building cars. The engines were manufactured by BMW engineers at another Munich plant and each one was extensively bench-tested. Then the cars were rigorously road-tested over a 40-kilometre (25-mile) route.

The cost at launch in September 1988 was a comparatively massive DM100,000, which made it over 50 per cent more expensive than the 535i. But each car and engine was hand-built (engines reputedly cost £8,000 each, or a quarter of the cost of the whole car).

It took more than a year for the M5 to arrive in Britain. When it went on sale in right-hand drive in February 1990, it cost £43,465, over £12,500 more than the otherwise range-topping 535i Sport. Imports were extremely restricted, only 189 being registered during 1990.

In the USA, the M5 was introduced for the 1991 model year, but with a lower maximum output of 310bhp. It lasted until 1993. Similarly, the Japanese-market M5 (offered from July 1991) was tightly emissions-restricted. BMW firmly resisted requests to fit an automatic transmission in either of these markets, which would also have been keen on another M5 development that, sadly, was abandoned.

In 1989, Motorsport engineers developed an M5 convertible, with two lengthened front doors and seating for four. It really did come very close to production – a price of £50,000 was agreed, and space was even booked at the Geneva motor show, but one week before its intended debut, BMW 'killed' it, believing it would have led to a demand for non-M 5 Series convertibles, which might have dented drop-top 3 Series sales.

At the end of 1991, the M5 went through its first major evolution. In response to criticisms that the M5 had not kept pace with advances in supercar performance – the Mercedes-Benz 500E was a notably powerful newcomer – the main brief was to enhance the already wide and strong torque band to increase performance, whilst simultaneously improving emissions. The M5's legendary throttle response also had to be retained.

In late 1991, the M5 was treated to its first major revisions. The engine grew in size to 3.8 litres and maximum power was extended to 340bhp – true supercar levels, and all from a six-cylinder engine. New external features were smart alloy wheels (with reverse-angled spokes claimed to have the same brake cooling effect as the previous design) and light-coloured aerodynamic aids.

The 1992 M5 featured Adaptive M Technic suspension, which was an automatic three-position damping system controlled by a highly sophisticated electronic brain. Both handling and ride quality improved.

In BMW's own words: "Only one thing can replace engine displacement: even more displacement." The familiar 'six' was stroked and bored so that the original 3,535cc grew to 3,795cc – another record-breaking size for a BMW 'six'. Wider ducts and valves on the intake side and larger exhaust valves improved efficiency, while new lightweight aluminium pistons enabled the compression ratio to rise to 10.5:1. Further improvements included solid-state high-tension ignition with six individual coils, more advanced Motronic 3.3 engine management, high-capacity M Power catalysation via two all-metal catalysts, a new larger-bore stainless steel exhaust manifold and improved water and oil cooling.

The clever electronic secondary throttle butterfly valve system was refined, being integrated within the overall engine management system. The results were a 14 per cent boost in torque (to 295lb.ft at 4,750rpm) and a 10 per cent rise in power (to 340bhp at 6,900rpm). Three-quarters of that torque was available from below 2,000rpm.

The desired effect was achieved: the 0-62mph time came down to just 5.9 seconds. The top speed could easily have exceeded 170mph had BMW not continued to limit it electronically to 155mph. Also, the spread of torque made the driving experience effortless when you wanted it. The power unit was even more smooth and serene in tone. It should be noted that the old 3.5-litre engine was kept in production alongside the new 3.8 engine until 1993.

The other main evolution for 1992 was Adaptive M Technic suspension, developed from that in the 7 Series. This EDCIII+ system was fully automatic, adjusting the dampers across three stages of tune. Various factors were fed into the electronic brain: road speed, vertical acceleration front and rear, and acceleration/deceleration. These determined what rate the Boge gas dampers should be set at, all at a very rapid pace. This made the M5 both tauter and more roll-free around bends and during fast acceleration or deceleration, yet superbly composed and comfortable at higher speeds on the straights.

It was not just the capacity which was enhanced on the 3.8-litre engine, but much of the internals: new aluminium pistons, more advanced engine management, bigger exhaust, better catalysation and a tweaked butterfly valve system. This was truly a state-of-the-art performance engine.

For the first time ever, BMW produced an M-badged estate car with the M5 Touring. Improbable amounts of luggage could now be transported at an unfeasibly rapid pace, and go-faster families with enthusiastic dog-owning drivers suddenly had a very satisfying motoring choice.

The spacious cabin of the M5 featured fully adjustable leather-edged seats, individual rear seats, lots of equipment and a speedometer calibrated to 300kmh (186mph). For 1992, the M5 interior was revamped as seen here with new Motorsport striped upholstery and Amaretta suede edging and headrests.

An optional 'Nürburgring' chassis package added a 1mm thicker rear anti-roll bar, 9in wide rear wheels with 255/40 ZR17 tyres, retuned Servotronic steering and a manually switchable version of the adaptive suspension.

Other minor changes to the 1992 M5 included a new lighter clutch and smoother low-speed gear-changing, and the abandonment of the finned wheel covers for attractive but more aggressive 8x17in five-spoke alloy wheels, still claimed to have the same cooling effect on the brakes. The interior was also upgraded, with a new Motorsport striped fabric finish in grey or black and 'easy-care' Amaretta suede-effect leather seat edging and headrests. Two new metallic colours were introduced: Avus Blue and Daytona Violet, and the discreet bodykit was now painted in a contrasting lighter colour.

For the first time ever there was a Touring version of the M5, 'Touring' being BMW's euphemism for an estate body. A prototype was shown at the Frankfurt show in September 1991 and it became available from spring 1992 in certain markets, but not, sadly, the UK. The Touring had the larger 9in wide rear wheels and 255-section tyres as standard (they were optional on the saloon). Because of its extra weight (80kg more at 1,730kg), performance and economy suffered a little. Despite the apparent contradictions of a nominal load-lugger capable of out-accelerating a Ferrari, the Touring immediately took around half of all M5 sales in Germany, proving that the major market for M5s consisted of people wanting discreet and practical, as well as extremely rapid, transport.

For the emissions-restricted Swiss and Austrian markets, the output of the 3.8-litre M5 dropped to 334bhp (and later 327bhp). The larger-engined M5 was not marketed in the USA, but a special 540i Sport model was launched there in 1995. This 200-off run-out E34 edition had the M5's suspension, brakes, wheels and bodywork modifications, allied to a 4-litre V8 engine.

A world first for BMW was the 1994 fitment of racing-style two-piece 'floating' disc brakes to the M5. These were perhaps the best brakes of any road car in their day.

For the last year of the M5's life, it was fitted with this new design of alloy wheel, which had now grown in diameter to 18 inches, 8in wide at the front and 9in wide at the back. The huge floating brake disc can be seen behind.

In September 1992, further changes were introduced as part of a scheme for the whole 5 Series. New standard features included an engine immobilizer, new door mirrors, side impact protection and seat belt pretensioners. Another range-wide inheritance was a driver's airbag, introduced in September 1993.

The last significant improvements arrived in May 1994, principally featuring that Nineties fad, a six-speed gearbox. Fifth and sixth were roughly equivalent to fourth and fifth in the old gearbox, and the spread of ratios below were ideally suited to getting the most out of changing gear. A higher final drive (3.23:1 instead of 3.91:1) also made cruising more comfortable (equating to 22.6mph/36.4kmh at 1,000rpm in fifth) and fuel economy remarkably impressive for a car of the M5's performance.

As for the brakes, the M5 became the first road car to use racing-style 'floating' disc brakes featuring multi-piece components. Separate friction rings ran in radial bearings, which were free to expand independently, thus avoiding disc distortion and extending life; they were also lighter. Also in 1994, the M5 gained new-style double-five-spoke 8x18in front and 9x18in rear wheels fitted with 245/40 ZR18 tyres, plus a slightly wider grille.

The M5 was officially retired in July 1995, just before the new-generation 5 Series arrived, and the following year BMW gave a green light to the development of the third-generation M5. Plans centred around a modified version of the 540i 32-valve V8 engine, expanded from 4.4 to 4.9 litres, bestowed with variable valve timing and said to be good for over 400bhp. This would make the M5 even quicker than the M3, and the most powerful road-going BMW ever. Expected launch date was summer 1998 and the new car, unlike the previous M5, was scheduled to be built on the regular 5 Series production line at Dingolfing, rather than hand-built at Garching.

CHAPTER 8

The svelte M635CSi

Quality without compromise – 1984-89

BMW's tradition of powerful coupes is an enviable one, stretching back to the earliest days. In the early 1970s, the BMW coupe ideal reached its zenith, the celebrated CSL becoming invincible on the track and an almost Wagnerian master on the road.

The car which was meant to succeed the CS was the 633CSi, launched in March 1976. This was a larger, more cossetting and more expensive Grand Tourer, which was extremely good at its job of whisking along the *autobahnen*. But frankly it was not a sportscar in the way that the CS series had been, lacking its taut handling and sporty feel.

Some attempt was made to redress this balance by fitting the venerable M49 3,453cc engine into the 6 Series in July 1978, creating the 635CSi. This engine was architecturally the same as that fitted to the M1, though it developed less power (218bhp). A far more sporting feel than the 633 was engendered by uprated dampers, springs and anti-roll bars, plus ventilated disc brakes.

It was really only a matter of time before BMW bit the bullet and fitted the full-house 24-valve M1 engine into the 635CSi. Naturally, the Motorsport division was given the development role. There was no problem fitting the M1 engine in place, although it had to be inclined at a 30-degree angle because of the flat front part. It shared the M1 specification very closely: light-alloy 24-valve head, twin overhead camshafts and central spark plugs. But it developed 9bhp more than the M1 engine, at 286bhp, due to new induction and twin-pipe exhaust systems and the use of Bosch Motronic II digital engine electronics; the radiator

was also bigger. The new engine transformed the 635CSi into a real M-class road-burner.

The standard transmission was a close-ratio Type 280/5 five-speed gearbox, beefed up for use in the M version, as was the clutch. The final drive was also rather lower than on other 6 Series models at 3.73:1 (optionally 3.91:1), and there was a 25 per cent limited-slip differential.

Of course, it was not all just about performance, and BMW Motorsport's expertise in the suspension department was given full rein. The M version had sports-tuned suspension with Bilstein gas-filled dampers, stiffer rear springs and beefed-up anti-roll bars. As a result, the car sat some 11mm (0.4in) lower than other 6 Series models. Also different were the aluminium wheels: very distinctive 165x390mm cross-spoke items with split rims (at least to begin with). Tyres were Michelin TRX 225/55 VR390, with an option of even wider 210x415mm wheels and 240/45 VR415 tyres. Additional steering castor was engineered in, and weight distribution was helped by resiting the (larger) battery to the boot.

Although the braking system, with servo-assisted discs all round, was based on that provided on other 6 Series models, for the M635CSi the single-piston calipers were swapped for four-piston items and the ventilated front discs were made 5mm thicker (to 30mm) and 18mm broader (to 300mm). Also, specially calibrated ABS was standard equipment.

The M635CSi weighed 1,510kg – making it the heaviest member of the 6 Series family – but it was endowed with

In 1983, the 6 Series became the first BMW to get the M1's legendary engine: the M635CSi was born. It may not have shared much else with the late, great M1, but it certainly traded off its heritage.

The M1 24-valve engine had to be inclined at an angle to fit under the 635's bonnet. It developed even more power than the M1 – 286bhp, an extra 9bhp – thanks to better piping and uprated electronics.

crushing performance: 0-100kmh was quoted as taking just 6.4 seconds, while the top speed was a phenomenal 158mph.

There was little to distinguish the M externally: just the wheels, the deeper front spoiler which jutted further forward, and Motorsport-coloured 'M' badges front and rear. A thicker M Style leather steering wheel told you you were in something special inside. Options included Recaro front seats, incorporating adjustable thigh support and leather trim. Otherwise, the M had all the gizmos associated with the 6 Series, including a service interval indicator, Active Check Control system, on-board computer, Energy Control fuel consumption display, electronically controlled automatic heater and electric sunroof.

The first showing of the M635CSi (some nicknamed it just M6) was at the September 1983 Frankfurt show, when Brabham-BMW Formula 1 driver Nelson Piquet gave it an enthusiastic introduction. Sales did not start, however, until April 1984. The extraordinary cost in Germany was DM89,500, almost DM22,000 more than for the 635CSi.

The M635CSi looked subtly more purposeful than other 6 Series cars: deep front spoiler, 'M' badging and distinctive split-rim cross-spoke alloy wheels. Although it was a heavy car, it performed extremely well: top speed was 158mph – after the M1, the highest maximum of any BMW, if only because electronic speed limiting had not yet become company policy. Not only was the M635CSi quick, it also handled with aplomb. Bilstein dampers, stiffer springing and thicker anti-roll bars saw to that.

Equipment levels reflected the M635CSi's status as BMW's top-of-the-range offering in the early 1980s, including an Active Check Control system, an on-board computer, automatic heater and electric sunroof. The speedometer read up to 280kmh (174mph).

Braking was also commensurate with the performance, thanks to thicker and wider discs, four-piston calipers and specially calibrated ABS. The 300mm front brakes are illustrated.

It was the same story when the M635CSi arrived in the UK in right-hand-drive form, in January 1985: at £32,195, the car was more expensive than a Ferrari 308GTS, and about the same as a Porsche 928. Not that it wasn't as capable, because it certainly was, but it just went to show that BMW's 6 Series was now moving in exalted company.

In October 1986, a catalyser became optional in some markets: power dropped to 260bhp and performance suffered, too (the top speed went down to 'only' 149mph). UK customers always made do without catalysts. The USA received its own version of the M model (always known simply as the M6) rather late in the day, in September 1986, as a 1987 model year car. It had a lower (9.8:1)

compression ratio and developed a less impressive 256bhp at 6,500rpm.

The following year (September 1987), in common with other 6 Series models, the M635CSi was given electric front seats (the driver's with memory settings), air conditioning and full leather trim (all 27 square metres of it!). Outside,

The seats in the M635CSi were both supportive and highly comfortable. As well as an automatic mechanism to allow easy entry, there was adjustability for rake, height and thigh cushion. These are the early-type seats – post-1987 ones were equipped with electronic controls.

The M635CSi did not become available in Britain in right-hand-drive form until 1985. It cost over £32,000, which made it more expensive than a Porsche 928. But with a claimed 0-60mph time of 6.1 seconds, it was definitely in the same league – and of course, it was much more rare and exclusive.

In 1987 there was a small facelift. The new energy-absorbing bumpers became body-coloured, the headlamps were now ellipsoid and the split-rim wheels were traded in for more conventional rims.

new colour-coded energy-absorbing bumpers and ellipsoid headlamps were shared with other 6 Series variants. Also gone were the split-rim wheels, replaced by one-piece alloy wheels with 8in wide rims and standard 245/45 VR415 tyres.

The M635CSi was kept in production alongside the standard 635CSi until February 1989, by which time 5,855 had been made. That would have been enough to homologate the M635CSi for racing, but by then it was well behind the competition and, in any case, the M3 had proven the ideal basis for racing, so the M635CSi never turned a wheel on the track, at least officially.

However, as a Grand Touring paragon, the M635CSi remains a genuine classic. As the flagship of the BMW range throughout the 1980s, it has retained considerable kudos. Also, it has seen no real successor: the 850i which succeeded it was far less sporting, and a planned M8 version of BMW's coupe for the 1990s remained stillborn.

The late-model M635CSi was considerably more luxurious than the earlier type, with its full leather interior, electrically-operated seats and air conidtioning.

Another exterior view of the same car. Note the protective cover which has been fitted over the side section of the rear bumper – a wise precaution if the car has to be parked in congested places.

CHAPTER 9

The exciting M Roadster

Transformation of the Z3 – from 1997

BMW sportscars have been rare but magnificent creatures. The glorious 507 of the 1950s was perhaps the apogee of BMW's sporting aspirations, a sensationally well proportioned V8-powered true sportscar, as scarce as it was rewarding to drive and own.

Perhaps it was back to that brief golden age that BMW wished to hark when plans were laid for a new sporting roadster in the 1990s. Apart from the marginal Z1 (only 8,093 of which were made between 1988 and 1991), there had been no BMW open sportscar since the 507.

The plan was certainly ambitious: to engineer a car from scratch and build it in a brand new factory in Spartanburg, South Carolina, USA. Yet it certainly paid off. Even before the car's official launch (in October 1995), posters advertising the new James Bond film *Goldeneye* showed exactly what was the secret agent's new transport – a Z3! Within 18 months, over 40,000 had been sold worldwide.

Initially, only 1.8 and 1.9-litre four-cylinder engines were available (only the 1.9 in the UK), while a 192bhp 2.8-litre six-cylinder unit was added to the range in 1996. But this was just the build-up to one of the most exciting sportscars the world has ever seen: the M Roadster.

The public first saw the M Roadster prototype at the Geneva motor show in March 1996, but it was a full year before the production-ready car was launched in earnest, the press being invited to Jerez in Spain to drive it just a few days before its official debut at the 1997 Geneva Salon. If the world had waited with baited breath for the Z3, the new M Roadster would surely take that breath away.

The basic recipe was predictable enough: take an M3 Evolution engine and put it under the Z3's long bonnet. The result was equally clear: here was a car which could accelerate from 0-100kmh in 5.4 seconds and power effortlessly up to an electronically-limited top speed of 155mph. The disappointing aerodynamics (a Cd of 0.41 was nothing to write home about) would have burdened the M Roadster much beyond this anyway.

The exhaust system was unique to the M Roadster, sharing the twin-catalyst layout of the M3, but exiting through four stainless steel tailpipes, two on each side of the car – purposeful-looking and delivering just the right noise. As for the gearbox, there was only enough space for the normal Z3 five-speed unit, not the six-speed 'box or sequential system of the M3, nor was an automatic possible.

No M car could escape without the M engineers working their chassis magic. Their task was certainly daunting: how to make a 1350kg rear-wheel-drive car, initially designed for only 140bhp, handle properly with more than double that power output. All the more remarkable is that they did it using nearly all existing components, chosen during extensive testing at the Nürburgring. The familiar Z3/Compact multi-link rear axle and semi-trailing arms were retained, but beefed-up with a new subframe claimed to be twice as strong as the old one (modified to fit a new 'short-neck' 3.15:1 final drive and differential oil cooler), reinforced trailing arms and anti-roll bars, recalibrated gas dampers and firmer springing. The whole front end came directly from the M3, complete with its tauter springs and

Starting with the extremely successful Z3 roadster, BMW M created a truly great sportscar with the M Roadster. The Z3 profile remained broadly identifiable, but virtually every aspect of its specification was changed.

Very fat wheelarches were an obvious sign that the Z3 had been given the M treatment. Other changes were a new front airdam with prominent wings at either end, restyled side strakes, white indicator lenses and aerodynamic door mirrors. The M Roadster certainly looked purposeful.

ZR17 rear). Combined with the quicker steering rack, the M Roadster became an endlessly enjoyable point-to-point machine.

Braking was equally mighty, thanks to the M3's contribution of its devastatingly effective compound discs and specially-matched Teves MkIV-G ABS system. The alloy wheels measured 7½ x17in at the front and 9 x17in at the back, and featured M5-style asymmetric metal humps which prevented the tyre bursting off the rim if punctured. The M Roadster was also the first BMW not to be fitted with a spare wheel, having instead a new M Mobility

Power came courtesy of the M3 Evolution: the 3.2-litre, 321bhp engine was transplanted without modification. However, there was simply not space for BMW to use the Evolution's six-speed gearbox, so the standard Z3 five-speed unit was fitted instead.

dampers, modified wheel geometry, altered stub-axle kinematics and reinforced spring plates. Ride height was 10mm lower than on other Z3 models.

Expert opinion judged the new M's road behaviour as outstanding. In all other Z3 variants, grip exceeded cornering forces in most circumstances. With the M Roadster, power oversteer was now readily available on demand – remember, no traction control was offered – and this was despite the very tenacious nature of the specially conceived Dunlop tyres (225/45 ZR17 front and 245/40

The huge M-branded alloy wheels (no less than 9in wide at the rear) were of different sizes front and rear. Together with the lack of space, this made carrying a spare wheel impractical, so BMW supplied a new M Mobility system – a can of sealant and a compressor to pump up the tyre.

The Z3's chassis was quite capable of coping with the 321bhp power output. Testers were struck by how entertaining the M car was compared with the over-grippy standard Z3. The quicker steering rack made life behind the wheel even more enjoyable.

The interior oozed class and 'retro' features: chrome-edged bezels, duo-tone leather trim, red needles for the dials, 'M Roadster' script on the rev-counter and M-branded steering wheel and gear-knob.

The Z3's superbly styled side cooling grilles deliberately evoked the style of the classic BMW 507. Hoods were colour-coordinated and electrically-operated, and the car looked every bit as good with the top raised as it did in pure roadster form.

The rear end was substantially reworked: a new bumper designed around quad-exit tailpipes and a resited number-plate, BMW badge and boot lock. Note the ellipsoid rear-view mirror. Roll-over hoops behind each seat were an evocative optional extra.

System developed in conjunction with Dunlop – a boot-mounted puncture sealant container and cigar lighter-activated compressor (and should the tyre be destroyed, BMW offered a special emergency replacement service).

While some thought the standard Z3 looked too wide at the front and perhaps a little insipid, no such doubts could be entertained about the M Roadster. It looked exactly right, with its massively wide five-spoked M RoadStar wheels sitting in fatter, reprofiled arches which increased overall width by 86mm (3.4in).

Both front and rear ends were restyled. The new front airdam (devoid of auxiliary lamps) boasted an aggressive shape and directed cooling air to the engine and rear axle, while twin 'tabs' enhanced downforce. At the back, the rear bumper was altered to accept the quadruple exhaust tailpipes; the number-plate also moved from the bumper onto the bootlid, the bootlid lock was repositioned and chromed, and the 'BMW' badge moved further up. Also, there were new restyled side air strakes with chrome grilles and 'M' logos – in this respect the style of the 507 was deliberately evoked. More 'M' badges appeared on the

Due for release in late 1997, the M version of the Z3 Coupe marked a new departure for BMW M GmbH. Here was a sports coupe/estate which would be competing head-on with Porsche, and it opened up new and exciting possibilites for the M division.

bootlid and door cutout trim. Other minor M traditions were adhered to: aerodynamic wing mirrors (with electric heating and adjustment) and white indicator lenses all round.

New paintwork schemes were available, including Imola Red, Kyalami Orange and Evergreen; optional metallic colours included Estoril Blue, Arctic Silver, Cosmos Black and Boston Green and, of course, BMW Individual would accommodate any other request. To match, the electrically folding roof was available in black, red or dark grey.

The standard nappa leather upholstery came in a choice of six colours. Duotoning was evident for the steering wheel, seats, door linings, storage compartment, centre console, windscreen surround and sun visors. The new heated seats were far more supportive than on other Z3 models, yet remained comfortable. Roll-bars behind the seats were an option.

The normal Z3 dials were treated to chrome bezels in the M Roadster (and naturally had red needles and 'M Roadster' branding). Even the door handles, gear-lever

gaiter surround and centre console heating/ventilation controls were chrome-edged, and three extra dials were provided on this console: clock, external temperature gauge and oil temperature. Other final touches included a new M steering wheel with airbag, an ellipsoid rear-view mirror and the M gear-knob.

Full production began in January 1997 at a planned rate of 2,200 per year. Right-hand-drive M Roadsters were expected to arrive in Britain in February 1998 at around the £40,000 mark – cheaper than an M3 Cabriolet. The final chapter in the M Roadster story was unfolding at the time this book was nearing completion, in May 1997, when BMW released its first pictures of the Z3 Coupe and confirmed that one version would have a full M specification: 3.2-litre engine giving 321bhp, fat wheelarches, M wheels and so on. It was scheduled to make its first official appearance at the Frankfurt show in September 1997 and its initial selling price in the UK was expected to be similar to that of the M Roadster, at around £40,000.

CHAPTER 10

Other M projects

The diversification of a letter

When BMW Motorsport GmbH was set up in 1972 as the racing wing of the Munich company, few could have imagined how far the organization would diversify. Special road car projects were the first departure, culminating in the M1 production supercar and the string of M models described in the preceding pages of this book.

But BMW M GmbH has become very much more than just a racing development and manufacturing operation, with the capacity to engineer and build special road cars. It now encompasses the disparate worlds of fashion, motorsport-inspired accessories, special trimming and driver training.

Almost from the start, BMW Motorsport catalogues offered performance-orientated parts for BMWs. But by the late 1970s, it was clear that there was a demand for other related products, and new phrases were coined for the operations into which BMW Motorsport began to diversify. There was M Power, the monicker which graced all Motorsport engines, road or race. M Technics covered technical components like aerodynamic aids, chassis tuning parts, wheels and tyres and so on. M Team was the racing department. M Style was the equivalent of merchandizing, offering branded fashion accessories. It became increasingly common to find standard BMWs being fitted with M Technics accessories, for example, and M-branded items found their way onto many higher-spec BMW production models.

The company-within-a-company has now developed wings within wings. From August 1, 1993, the Motorsport name was officially changed so that the company became known simply as BMW M GmbH. It was split into three different areas: BMW M Cars, BMW Individual and BMW Driver Training.

BMW M Cars speaks for itself. Individual was set up in 1992 as an all-new branch of the operation. Prior to this official status, BMW Motorsport had provided a bespoke trimming and specification service for M cars, but from 1992 it also catered for personalizing standard BMWs. This was not merely fitting options from a list, it was a complete accommodation of a customer's individual wishes.

So at BMW Individual, one might expect to find a bright purple 325i sitting alongside a Cabriolet being converted to a yellow leather/carbon-fibre interior, a Compact being fitted with a full-length fabric sunroof, a 750iL being fitted with big alloy wheels and a fax machine, and an 8 Series being colour-coded. As well as a list of exclusive items like special steering wheels and gear-knobs, BMW Individual would also manufacture unique items to special order.

BMW Driver Training has had its home at Motorsport headquarters since 1976. Experienced instructors aim to teach drivers how to handle their BMWs with the utmost safety, present information on vehicle dynamics, run winter driving courses, offer high-speed training in M3s and also run group training. In 1996 alone, over 8,400 drivers participated in BMW Driver Training.

Semi-M projects, such as the Italian 320iS and South African 333i, have already been noted in the relevant chapters, but one further M-related project should be

noted. The South African 745i, a unique model produced in the mid-1980s, was fitted with a pukka M635CSi engine, quite different from the German-made 745i, and was capable of over 150mph – which made it the fastest BMW then in production.

It was also to the Motorsport division that BMW turned when criticisms of its 850i flagship coupe needed to be addressed. At the Paris Salon of October 1992, BMW launched the 850CSi, which had been comprehensively reworked and tuned by BMW M. The Motorsport team heavily revised the V12 engine, increasing the capacity from 4,988cc to 5,576cc and fitting new pistons, a stronger crank, hotter cam profiles, a new intake manifold, revised engine management and an oil cooler. Power went up from 300 to 380bhp, transforming the previously lukewarm performance. The engine received a 'Powered by M' casting in recognition. BMW M also fitted an oil-cooled differential, a beefed-up clutch and M5 steering (including steering rear wheels). It also altered the suspension significantly: there was a reinforced front axle with bigger

wheel bearings and hydraulic mounting points, and revised anti-roll bars, springs and dampers, while the brakes were uprated. The car sat lower, had a new airdam, twin exhaust tailpipes, typical M ellipsoid door mirrors, M alloy wheels, and more leather trim. The result was a car which neared a true M-specification product – indeed, BMW M GmbH does regard it as an M car – but the 8 Series was still fundamentally flawed at root.

The 850CSi is perhaps best regarded as a consolation project for BMW M, since at one stage there was to have been a pukka M8. Development of this project began in 1990, and by 1991 a fully functioning prototype had been built, with the firm intention to put it into production. The 5-litre V12 engine was upgraded in a series of prototypes, ranging from a 400bhp 5.1-litre unit up to a monstrous 6-litre 600bhp version (which was used as the first testbed for the McLaren V12). The intended production engine grew to 5.4 litres, received quad cams and 48 valves, and could produce 500bhp, while the torque was so high that a five-speed gearbox was used instead of the usual 850i six-

After the failure of a project to produce an M8 version of the 8 Series, BMW M GmbH did the technical work to bring the 850CSi to reality. This included the engine, suspension, steering, brakes and cosmetics. Motorsport also built the 850CSi at its factory.

The coveted 'M' casting was worn by the 850CSi V12 engine in recognition of the heavy modifications it had undergone. Compared with the old 850i unit, power shot up 80bhp to 380bhp.

speeder. Weight was reduced by making the doors and bonnet out of Kevlar and the windows out of plastic, and the rear seats were thrown away. Bodywork modifications included a deep front airdam, different headlamp treatment, blistered wheelarches with airdams in the rear pair for oil coolers, extended skirts, a lower rear valance, aerodynamic door mirrors, a vaned bonnet and much wider wheels and tyres.

This was to be an all-out supercar with a potential top speed of 188mph, sub-5-second 0-60mph acceleration and flexible torque characteristics, active rear-wheel steering and yet surprising refinement, all at a cost of around £100,000. But it was never to be: Wolfgang Rietzle, then head of BMW Research and Development, vetoed the idea of even just a small run of M8 cars, to be produced by BMW Motorsport. With the comment: "We're just not interested in putting our name to cars like these any more," he pulled the plug on the M8. The M8 project engineer added: "The old animals are dead. The M8 is not a car for our time." Details of the project were given to the press in the spring of 1991 to quell definitively speculation that such a car might enter production.

But just as the M8 project was being stamped on, BMW Motorsport gained a new – and possibly even more exciting

The fabulous V12 engine developed by BMW M Power for McLaren's F1 road car was a pinnacle of the art. Compact, lightweight, hugely powerful, tractable, reliable and simply beautiful to look at.

– project towards which to redirect its talents. Ron Dennis – already well-known to BMW through his campaigning of the championship-winning M1 in the Procar series of 1979 – was now managing director of the TAG McLaren Group, which included the hugely successful Formula 1 team. Another McLaren man with strong BMW connections was Gordon Murray, who had been chief engineer and designer at Brabham during the years when BMW was supplying it with F1 engines. Between them, they conceived the now-celebrated McLaren F1 road car.

For the very special V12 engine which they knew they would need for what was to be the fastest road car on earth

they turned to Paul Rosche, at BMW Motorsport. The deal was signed in February 1991 and work began the following month. Amazingly, by Christmas the same year, BMW was testing its first built-up engine, and by March 1992 it had supplied one to McLaren for testing in its prototype.

Its essentials make fascinating reading. The so-called S70/2 all-aluminium engine had a V12 format, dry-sump lubrication, a displacement of 6.1 litres, a power output of 627bhp (and therefore well over 100bhp per litre), 500lb.ft of torque (398lb.ft of which was available at just 1,500rpm), a compact 600mm block length and an overall weight of just 266kg. That sounds like a thoroughbred racing engine, yet

Arguably the ultimate expression of M Power. The lucky driver of a McLaren F1, whose central driving position is flanked by a pair of passenger seats slightly to the rear of him, can sample the performance of BMW's specially developed 6-litre V12 engine, though 627bhp, 500lb.ft of torque and a top speed of around 230mph are the sort of figures normally associated with the race track. Equally important, therefore, is this remarkable engine's ability to allow the McLaren to be driven along in top gear at a mere trickle without protesting.

the truth was that this had to be a tractable unit for everyday use in all conditions, and BMW's achievement in this respect cannot be underestimated. Much of the technology came from other engines: for example, the VANOS variable timing system was closely related to that on the M3 (although the angle of valve overlap was much higher than the M3's). The specification was nothing if not impressive:

Capacity: 6,064cc
Cylinders: 12 in 60-degree vee
Bore x stroke: 86 x 87mm
Valves: four per cylinder, DOHC, infinitely variable valve timing

Compression ratio: 10.5:1 (or 11.0:1)
Power output: 627bhp at 7,400rpm (609bhp in some markets)
Torque: 500lb.ft at 5,600rpm (480lb.ft in some markets)

Naturally, the V12 had to conform to emissions standards. As with the M5, secondary air injection reduced emissions during warm-up, and no less than four catalysts did the job of removing pollutants. Twin Lucas injectors supplied fuel to each cylinder in sequential form, carefully controlled by a fantastically complex engine management system. Each cylinder also had its own ignition coil, as in the M5, and a 'hot wire' sensor system was used.

The only exotic material used in the predominantly

aluminium and steel powerplant was the Inconel stainless steel chosen for the exhaust system and the titanium for the silencer.

In so-called GTR form, for racing, the stroke was shortened to bring the engine displacement below 6 litres (5,991cc) and, ironically, the power output was actually fractionally less than on the road version of the F1, although torque was higher.

The roadgoing F1 weighed only 1,140kg and so the 627bhp BMW engine (it wore both 'McLaren' and 'BMW M Power' script) was capable of providing crushing performance: over 230mph top speed, 0-60mph in 3.2 seconds, 50-70mph in 3.7 seconds and 0-200mph in 28 seconds. On the latest information, a mere 100 McLaren F1s were scheduled to be built, making both the car and the BMW engine amongst the rarest pieces of automotive machinery on the planet: a fitting testament to the pinnacle of their respective fields.

BMW Driver Training was another part of M GmbH, and aimed to place and evaluate drivers behind the wheel of an M3 in high-speed situations, among other disciplines.

CHAPTER 11

M stands for Motorsport

The BMWs in competition

BMW's history is rich in competition glory, but since this book deals specifically with the era of BMW Motorsport (from 1972 onwards), this chapter confines itself to these years; for BMW achievements prior to this date, please refer back to Chapter 1.

When BMW Motorsport GmbH was created in 1972 as a company-within-a-company, its brief was to run and maintain BMW's entire racing programme. Jochen Neerpasch joined BMW in May that year to take charge of what would become a formidable force across a wide field of motorsports. He had joined BMW from Ford, where he had enjoyed spectacular success running that company's European Touring Car effort: the Capri RS romped home with the 1971 driver's title. Now, the young Neerpasch was out to beat the team he had nursed to victory.

He took over as Competitions Director after a lull in BMW's racing programme, the BMW board having pulled the plug on its Formula 2 effort in 1970. But with Neerpasch on board, BMW was once again making a firm commitment to racing, most visibly by founding BMW Motorsport GmbH. Neerpasch had also brought Martin Braungart with him from Ford as his number two.

Although 1972 went decisively Ford's way (there was no BMW works ETC team in 1972, only the Schnitzer and Alpina-backed teams of CS Coupes), 1973 would prove to be BMW's year. Helped by a massive injection of finance from the board, BMW looked a formidable force, but the thing which sealed Neerpasch's triumph was a clever reading of the rules regarding aerodynamic aids. In mid-season, just before the cut-off date for homolgation of modifications, BMW fitted a kit of aerodynamic spoilers to its CSLs, creating the now celebrated 'Batmobile'. Martin Braungart was responsible for effecting the aerodynamic wings which made the BMW CSL invincible that year: a deep front spoiler, boot spoiler, roof spoiler and rubber wing fins. BMW had an instant aerodynamic advantage, and it was too late for Ford to reply. BMW took the manufacturer's title by six rounds to two, and the Dutch BMW driver Toine Hezemans scooped the driver's title.

That was the first outright win for BMW in ETC racing and, incidentally, the first year in which BMW's new blue, violet and red Motorsport livery was used. Ford fought back the following year to win the driver's title in a season dominated by the Suez-provoked oil crisis and consequent cost-cutting. The 1974 Nurburgring event was the last works event for Group 2 CSLs (although the CSL would continue to be campaigned successfully in IMSA racing in America). Private teams also continued to rack up CSL victories in the Touring Car stakes: Sigi Muller and Alan Peltier won in 1975, Pierre Dieudonne and Jean Xhevencal triumphed in '76, Dieter Quester in '77 and Umberto Grano in '78.

BMW's works effort, meanwhile, was switched to the more spectacular Group 5. Porsche was absolutely dominant in this series with its turbocharged 935, against which the normally-aspirated BMWs were outclassed. But a turbocharged CSL – with 750bhp on tap – looked as though it might offer a challenge when it was first raced at

The 3.0 CSL was absolutely dominant for BMW in ETC racing in the 1970s, and established the newly-formed BMW Motorsports division as a force with which to be reckoned.

Paul Rosche became General Manager of Motorsport and went on to develop racing versions of the 3 Series and M3, and to originate BMW's successful Formula 1 engine programme.

Silverstone in May 1976 with Ronnie Peterson and Gunnar Nilsson at the helm. But despite an excellent start, the gearbox was simply not up to the task of handling the huge amount of power and the CSL lost its lead.

Also in 1976, the new BMW 3 Series was given its first taste of competition. In 1975, engineer Paul Rosche had become General Manager of BMW Motorsport, in charge of engine development, and it was he who evolved the racing 3 Series. This was earmarked to be campaigned by the works team in the German national championship in Group 5 under the 'BMW Junior Team' banner, with young drivers Eddie Cheever, Manfred Winkelhock and Marc Surer driving. The racing was spectacular, and at times out-of-control!

BMW also fielded the 320i in World Championship Group 5 events, and although everyone concerned knew they were never likely to be in contention for the outright title, a 320i did win the 2-litre class two years running. Other 3 Series successes were scored in IMSA, where turbocharged cars competed in North America (and where British driver David Hobbs notched up four race victories and finished third overall in the 1979 series); and with Schnitzer-developed 410bhp 1.4-litre turbo cars in the German national championship (in which Harald Ertl won

Harald Ertl won the German national title in 1978 in this radical Schnitzer-prepared BMW 320 Turbo.

This BMW Italia-entered 635CSi took the pairing of Helmut Kelleners and Umberto Grano to a 1981 European Touring Car Championship victory. The later M version of the 635CSi was not produced in sufficient quantity to homologate it for racing.

the 1978 title and roundly beat the works 2-litre cars).

Another area of BMW Motorsports activity was Formula 2. BMW revisited this class in 1973 when it began supplying engines to March and others, and Jean-Pierre Jarier took the title in convincing style, the first of a string of March-BMW Formula 2 victories in 1974 (Patrick Depailler), 1975 (Jacques Laffite in a Martini-BMW), 1978 (Bruno Giacomelli), 1979 (Marc Surer) and 1982 (Corrado Fabi).

By then, BMW had already courted the rarified world of Formula 1. The company had initiated the development of a 1.5-litre turbocharged engine, and Jochen Neerpasch saw this as the ideal basis for an M Power F1 platform. He actually negotiated a deal with the Brabham team to supply this engine for the 1980 season, but the BMW board vetoed the idea and Neerpasch ended up leaving BMW and joining Talbot. He had wanted to take the engine project with him, but his deputy at BMW, Dieter Stappert, stepped into his shoes as Competitions Director and resisted the move. So BMW kept its Formula 1 engine programme.

Paul Rosche did the development work, creating the M12/13 1.5-litre turbo 'four'. Brabham ran the engines in 1981, but did not actually compete with them until 1982, when Nelson Piquet scored the first victory for a BMW-engined F1 car at the Canadian Grand Prix. The following season, he became the first driver to win the World Championship at the wheel of a turbocharged car when he and his Brabham-BMW scored a narrow points victory over Alain Prost and his Renault.

This was undoubtedly the high point of BMW's F1 involvement, although the company continued to supply engines to the Brabham team until 1987, and to Arrows until 1988. The last recorded BMW-powered Formula 1 race win was Gerhard Berger's victory for Benetton at the 1986 Mexican Grand Prix. However, that may not necessarily have been the final F1 chapter for BMW since it has been widely rumoured that the company has been engaged on the design and development of a Formula 1 engine following confirmation that the current 3-litre rules will remain in force well into the next millenium.

Perhaps the most important chapter in BMW

Jochen Neerpasch might well smile in the presence of Niki Lauda: his M1 had just been saved from the competitive wilderness by the idea of a Procar series run alongside Formula 1 events.

Motorsport's history was provided by the M1, for a variety of reasons. Production of the M1 had begun in September 1978, and BMW was faced with an extremely embarrassing situation: the M1 simply stood no chance of being homologated. Jochen Neerpasch had conceived the car to compete with Porsche in Group 5, but rule changes meant it would never be homologated in that category, and equally, if it was to compete in Group 4, it would first be necessary to build 400 cars. So what could BMW do with its newly-born supercar?

It was Max Mosley who proved to be the M1's saviour. As one of the senior players in the Formula One Constructors' Association (FOCA), Mosley came up with the idea of running a Procar series exclusively for the M1 as a supporting event alongside F1 Grands Prix. Understandably, Neerpasch was very enthusiastic because it would mean that BMW would have a presence at F1 events, and even have a selection of F1 drivers at the wheel of its cars, without the huge expense of becoming directly involved with Formula 1 itself. For Mosley, the attraction was that it would provide an entertaining extra event at F1 meetings and the opportunity to get F1 drivers back into some production car racing.

The plan was to run the M1 Procar races after the last practice session for each of the eight European Grands Prix in the 1979 season. The first five places on the grid would be reserved for the top five F1 drivers in practice, the remainder of the 25-strong field being composed of private entrants. Points would be awarded in each race for the top 10 placings (on a scale of 20-15-12-10-8-6-4-3-2-1). Prizes at each event were to be $5,000 for first place, $3,000 for second and $1,000 for third, the overall winner at the end of the season receiving a brand new M1; second place would be rewarded with a BMW 528i and third place with a 323i.

As an inducement to persuade rival teams to let their drivers be seen racing in a BMW, similar prizes were also offered to the F1 teams. But despite this coaxing, several teams insisted on adhering to the terms of their supplier contracts. At the first Procar event, at the 1979 Belgian Grand Prix meeting, it was actually BMW's choice of Goodyear tyres which threw a spanner in the works. Michelin-contracted drivers from the Ferrari and Renault

The closely-bunched field of 20 M1s just after the startline during the 1979 Procar series made an impressive spectacle. Reliability problems early on and strong opinions about the relevance of the series fuelled the M1 controversy.

The thinking man's supercar would be an accurate description of the M1, the first road-going car to bear the M badge of BMW Motorsport. Not only did it have fine handling balance and. a very powerful race-derived engine, it was far more practical and far better built than any other car in its class. A mere 450 were made between 1979 and 1981.

Putting a BMW 635CSi engine into the modest looking 5 Series bodyshell created, in 1979, one of the world's best Q cars: the M535i. An upgraded interior, wider alloy wheels, badging and spoilers were the only clues that this was anything special – and it certainly was, boasting a top speed of 138mph.

Hans Stuck leads Niki Lauda during a 1979 Procar race – but not for long, as Lauda ran away with the title that year. Both drivers had arranged deals to race private cars, which battled it out with the five top-qualifying Formula 1 drivers on the grid.

In the 1980 series, Nelson Piquet proved victorious. Here he chases the field in a works car which has apparently lost one of its rear wheelarches.

Outside the Procar series, the M1 was not as competitive as BMW would have wished. One encouraging result was a third placing for Stuck/Piquet at the Nürburgring 1000kms in 1980.

teams were prevented from racing, so the two fastest qualifiers (Gilles Villeneuve for Ferrari and Jean-Pierre Jabouille for Renault) were unable to race the M1s. Eventually, drivers were taken from as far down the field as eighth: the five who took part were Jacques Laffite, Clay Regazzoni, Mario Andretti, Niki Lauda and Nelson Piquet.

Niki Lauda was certainly in the best position to win the title that year. He had arranged a deal to drive an M1 for the season through Ron Dennis' Marlboro-backed Project 4 group, so even if he failed to qualify as one of the fastest F1 drivers, he would still get a drive. Predictably, Lauda won the title in 1979.

Perhaps because of the spectacular success of the series, clinched from the jaws of an embarrassing no-man's-land, the Procar series was overshadowed by adverse comment. It had gained a reputation as the most expensive one-make category in the world: although race cars cost a not unreasonable £40,000 each, it cost all of £120,000 to keep one car going for a full season. There were also some early reliability problems, leading to the first event at Zolder

descending into near-farce. Some FOCA members were not too keen on BMW hitching a ride on the F1 circuit, either, as Ken Tyrrell asserted: "BMW should build an F1 car if they want to get in on Grand Prix racing" – a prophetic judgment as it turned out!

The sport's governing body, FISA, also labelled the series a 'non-serious' form of motorsport, viewing it as a mere publicity exercise. The French federation even tried to ban Procar racing at the 1979 French Grand Prix meeting, provoking a row with FOCA boss Bernie Ecclestone. Nevertheless, despite the controversy, the Procar series was run again the following year on the same basis, and this time Brabham driver Nelson Piquet won the title. However, by then the Procar series had run its course and the idea was quietly retired.

It had been intended that an M1 should run at Le Mans, naturally in a more radically modified Group 5 form, and it was mooted to have a twin-turbo version of the six-cylinder engine, developing around 800bhp. Top speed would have been around 220mph. However, fate intervened and the

The already very capable BMW 6 Series was turned into one of the world's best Grand Touring cars when BMW Motorsport worked its magic to create the M635CSi. Not only did it have more power than the M1 (286bhp), its enhanced suspension, transmission and braking gave it peerless dynamic prowess for a four-seater.

Understatement personified: the 1984-88 M5 looked very little different from any other current 5 Series model. Under the skin, however, it was pure Motorsport: 286bhp engine, bigger brakes, upgraded suspension, quicker steering and a close-ratio gearbox. It had the distinction of being exclusively hand-built by dedicated Motorsport staff.

An output of 600bhp from 1,499cc: this was BMW's M Power turbocharged Formula 1 engine, which took Nelson Piquet to the F1 World Championship in 1983.

M1 would never be eligible for Group 5 because of the homologation rule changes. Consequently, the sole car prepared for Le Mans had to be entered as a Group 6 car. Herve Poulain, Marcel Mignot and Manfred Winkelhock shared the driving, and despite having to cope with a persistent misfire, they still managed to finish sixth, which was the only real success for the M1 that year. This car was later reworked by March Engineering for BMW North America to race in the IMSA series, but it had little success there.

The M1 failed to make much impact in other events. In 1980, sixth place was gained in the Mugello 6 Hours, with Didier Pironi and Dieter Quester driving, but perhaps the M1's best result that year was third in the Nürburgring 1000kms, when Hans Stuck and Nelson Piquet drove their car exceptionally well. At Le Mans, 14th place was all the Pironi/Quester/Mignot M1 could muster, with the M1 of Stuck/Berger/Lacaud immediately behind it. A French team also fielded an M1 in tarmac rallying, but with little success.

Thereafter the M1 became even more outclassed and so it faded quickly from the racing scene.

BMWs, however, continued to exert their dominance of the European Touring Car Championship. For 1982, the works team's contender was the 528i, developing 240bhp. It looked outclassed but, in the hands of Helmut Kelleners and Umberto Grano, it took the drivers' title that season. By then, the big V12 TWR Jaguar XJS was proving a real threat, and so BMW moved back to the larger and more powerful 635CSi Coupe, a Schnitzer-prepared car proving good enough for Dieter Quester to earn his fourth ETC title in 1983. Jaguar won the following year, and the ideal response would have been a racing M635CSi, but Group A homologation rules required a run of 5,000 cars and the specialized M635CSi was never likely to sell in sufficient quantities for quick homologation. But there was more to come from the 635CSi: Schnitzer's car won at the Spa 24 Hours in 1986, Dieter Quester, Altfried Heger and Thierry Tassin being the victorious drivers, and the sister car of

The M3 became BMW's track weapon from 1987 through into the 1990s. Roberto Ravaglia (seen here in action at Hockenheim) won the inaugural – and last – World Touring Car title in 1987, starting a cascade of victories for the M3.

Roberto Ravaglia, Gerhard Berger and Emanuele Pirro came in third. Ravaglia also secured the driver's title in the 1986 ETC in a 635CSi.

In 1987 came BMW's next great hope for glory: the M3. Unlike BMW's previous track contenders, the M3 was created specifically as a competition car. BMW was certainly optimistic about the model's potential, but even it could not have predicted its degree of success in translating that potential into the most spectacular competition record of any BMW ever – indeed, the most successful saloon car in recent history. On the track (and even, to some extent, in rallying) the M3 became almost invincible for years to come. As described in Chapter 3, Thomas Ammerschlager engineered the M3 chassis and Paul Rosche created a brilliant new 2.3-litre four-cylinder powerplant by slicing the end off an M1 cylinder head and mating it to a modified BMW slant-four iron block.

Racing M3s differed from road cars in a number of important respects. Of course, the weight went down (to 960kg/2,116lb) but that lower weight was also perfectly distributed 50/50 front to rear. As well as having a rollcage and a racing fuel tank, the M3 was stripped of its power steering and given a quicker rack, reinforced semi-trailing arms, adjustable anti-roll bars, modified Bilstein aluminium spring struts with adjustable spring plates, new hubs, a 40mm/1.6in lower ride height, modified Motronics EMS, special racing gearboxes, uprated brakes and single-nut three-piece 9x17in wheels. Engine capacity typically was slightly bigger at 2,332cc (thanks to a small increase in bore), meaning an initial output of around 300bhp, which would rise to as high as 365bhp by 1991.

Roberto Ravaglia won the inaugural World Touring Car title in 1987, a series being dominated by BMW; it was certainly not a disadvantage that Munich had weighted the odds with a massive investment of cash. Its other drivers that year were Ivan Capelli, Roland Ratzenberger and Emanuele Pirro. Similarly, BMW dominated the ETC Group A Championship in 1987, Winni Vogt coming home first, with little opposition from other teams. These were merely the two most coveted crowns of a whole clutch of

The original M3 remains one of the true motoring legends. Its level of driver involvement has hardly been bettered, thanks to a brilliant chassis, raw four-cylinder engine and keenly focussed specification. This is the ultimate Sport Evolution, a 600-off homologation edition with more power and an additional adjustable wing on the rear spoiler.

BMW has never forgotten its motorsports heritage, which stretches right back to the 328. The 1992 M3 carried forward the sporting mantle but was a very different car from the previous M3, having a more refined six-cylinder engine, more forgiving handling and extra comfort. Its performance and road behaviour placed it firmly in the supercar category.

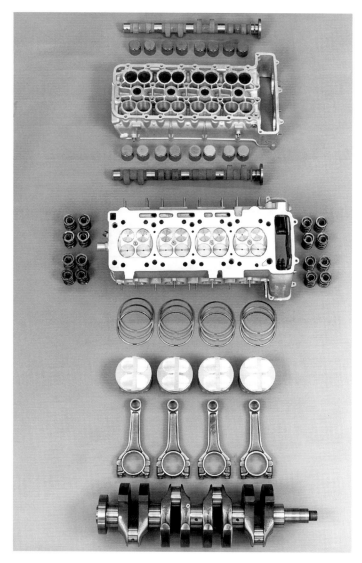

Group A M3 2.3-litre engines featured these special components, which boosted power as high as 300bhp.

worldwide championships in the M3's debut year: its other spoils were the European Hillclimb and Touring Car titles in Germany, Australia, France, Finland, the Netherlands and Portugal.

Rallying was never works-supported by BMW, but the M3 suddenly looked to have good potential after the demise of the mighty Group B monsters in 1986. Despite the fact that the M3 would always be at a disadvantage because it lacked four-wheel drive, the British team Prodrive took on the task of developing a convincing rally contender with a 285bhp, six-speed car. On the World Championship tarmac route of the 1987 Tour de Corse, Bernard Beguin beat works-backed Audi Quattros, Lancia Integrales and Ford Sierra Cosworths to take the most memorable rally victory for the M3. The Corsican victory had followed by just two weeks the first blood of the season, Beguin's victory in the Rallye Touraine, which was part of the French Championship.

In successive years, small but significant aerodynamic enhancements were incorporated into the M3, as detailed in Chapter 3. Racing M3s also benefited from even larger 18in diameter wheels, lighter body panels and ever-increasing power outputs.

For the M3, 1988 would prove just as good a year as its first. In the last European Touring Car Championship of all, Roberto Ravaglia beat the Ford Sierra Cosworths to take the title (a feat which led BMW to offer a limited-edition road-going M3 called the Europa Meister). Other ETC M3 drivers that year included Winni Vogt and Jacques Laffite.

The M3 had its first taste of British Touring Car success in 1988, when BMW dealer Frank Sytner won the title in a Prodrive car (while injury prevented radio DJ Mike Smith from making much impression the same year). It would be 1991 before the M3 secured this title again, when Will Hoy triumphed in a Vic Lee Motorsport-prepared car. British cars had to run to a 2-litre limit to conform with local regulations, which was achieved by shortening the stroke of the engine (reducing power to 270bhp as a result).

Other spoils in 1988 included Touring Car titles in the national series of France, the Netherlands, Portugal, Sweden, Italy, Norway, Spain and Asia-Pacific. In rallying,

The M3 pilot was ensconced within a substantial roll-cage and had full racing controls. Note that the dashboard and door trims remained almost as they were on the roadgoing M3.

Francois Chatriot took fourth place on the 1988 Tour de Corse, and would later go one better, securing third places in both 1989 and 1990. A Prodrive M3 also won the 1988 Belgian rally title and came second in the European Rally Championship – infuriatingly close to a European racing/rallying double.

At European Championship level, rallying M3s were remarkably successful considering the disadvantage of rear-wheel drive, winning eight events in 1988, five in 1989 and three more in 1990, showing a picture of understandably diminishing success. The five 1989 national titles were in France, Belgium, the Netherlands, Yugoslavia and Spain, and 1990 brought one further French title to the already well-stocked trophy cabinet.

After disappointment in 1988, the 1989 German Championship went BMW's way again, with Roberto Ravaglia in the hot seat, this despite the fact that Mercedes-Benz's 190E had a larger 2.5-litre engine. Five other national titles went to the M3 that year, including Johnny Cecotto's in Italy. But for 1990, BMW homologated the 2.5-litre Sport Evolution in order to defend its German title. Engine capacity was slightly larger than for the road-going Sport Evolution (2,493cc instead of 2,467cc) and

performance was notably improved in the mid-range. But there was a new challenge in 1990: the four-wheel-drive Audi V8, which took the title that and the following year. Meanwhile, Roberto Ravaglia added an Italian Championship to his German title in 1989.

In 1990, the M3 pulled off a dramatic 1-2 win at the Spa 24 Hours, the winning car being piloted by Johnny Cecotto, Fabien Giroix and Markus Osterreich. Other 1990 achievements included national titles in France, Italy, Holland, Switzerland, Finland and Belgium, plus the European Hillclimb Championship for the third time (M3s would win it six times in total). Also, M3s came second in the British and German series (Johnny Cecotto being the driver in the latter).

By 1991, it had been calculated that over 330 competition M3s had been sold – a remarkable total, especially considering that the 1991 price tag was £90,000 without an engine or gearbox, or £140,00 with the power train installed. Such sales greatly boosted the turnover and staffing of BMW Motorsport GmbH, and fully justified its expansion into the new Garching site in 1986.

Another near-miss for the M3 came in 1991 when Steve Soper finished third in the driver's championship in

As well as a convertible M3, BMW produced a four-door saloon version, which epitomized the phrase 'wolf in sheep's clothing'. Here was a 155mph full five-seater which looked almost as modest as a 316i. This is the 1996 Evolution model with an even more powerful 321bhp 3.2-litre six-cylinder engine.

With the 1988-95 M5, BMW reached a true pinnacle. This was probably the most complete car then being made, incredibly powerful and rewarding to drive, yet at the same time docile, understated and practical. Small wonder that it received a surfeit of accolades from the press. The example pictured is one ot the last six-speed M5s off the Motorsport production line.

Germany and BMW finished in second in the constructor's stakes behind Mercedes-Benz. It racked up successes in the ETC and eight national championships.

By 1992, the new E36 3 Series was well and truly established, and the old M3 was looking long-in-the-tooth. However, the old-shape car did carry on for one last season, and the list of triumphs stacked up: M3s won national titles in Germany, the Netherlands, Luxembourg, Austria, Sweden and Spain.

However, in Britain, the Touring Car challenge was taken up by the new 318iS (not the M3 as it was beyond the 2-litre limit), but BMW was outclassed that year by the Vauxhall Cavaliers and Toyota Carinas. In 1993, the 318i was far more on the pace: Steve Soper joined the British BTC challenge and was a very close runner-up to Joachim Winkelhock, also in a Team Schnitzer-prepared BMW. Soper was also runner-up in the second Touring Car World Cup at Donington in 1994 – by just two seconds behind Paul Radisich's Ford Mondeo – Jo Winkelhock picking up third in the other BMW 318i. Thereafter, BMW struggled in BTCC and eventually withdrew from the series altogether.

The new-shape E36 M3 was homologated for racing for the 1993 season. BMW's list of successes continued, but the prestigious German title slipped through its fingers. By 1994 the 318iS was making most of the running in BMW's motorsport programme – and with great success – but in many events the M3 continued its run of victories unabated.

Indeed, in 1995 the E30 M3 was still capable of winning the European Hillclimb Championship, the Touring Car Trophies of Germany, Luxembourg and Hungary, and a Nürburgring event. The E36 M3 won the ADAC GT Cup (Division 2) and, in America, the SCCA Showroom Stock Car title. Even the M5 got a look-in in 1995: Shawn Hendricks took the IMSA Super Car series. In 1996, the Italian TC series was won by Roberto del Castello in an M3, the ADAC Cup again went Marc Simon's way, the all-woman team of Rafanelli/Surer/Duez won Group N at the Spa 24 Hours, and Reck/Scheidd/Widmann won the Nürburgring 24 Hours.

In the history of BMW's mastery of the Touring Car artform and its surprising success in rallying, the Motorsports division can take the credit for making the major progress. In particular, the Motorsport-developed M3 has now passed into the book of motorsport legends as probably the world's most successful single racing saloon.

CHAPTER 12

Buying and owning an M car

The choice, the inspection and the cost

Motorsport-badged BMWs represent the pinnacle of an already prestigious brand. As such, all examples attract significant premiums over the standard production models on which they were based, as befits a range of models carrying the 'M' logo. These cars are engineered in a different way from mainstream BMWs and in certain cases, such as the M5, were even hand-built on separate Motorsport production lines.

Rarity is both the attraction and the curse for the prospective buyer. With the exception of the new-shape M3, every used M-badged car is available only in very limited supplies. The best place to start is probably one of the specialist BMW clubs, since most M cars are owned by enthusiasts who are likely to be club members. Another good source, of course, is one of the many specialist BMW dealers.

Expense is the other main ownership factor. It is not so much the purchase cost – used M cars can be picked up for surprisingly little outlay these days – as the subsequent cost of ownership. Insurance, servicing, parts and fuel all play their part, although compared to many other high-performance cars and supercars, the costs are not prohibitive.

Generally speaking, the parts situation is excellent. Such optimism might not apply to the prices you have to pay, but BMW and a host of specialists are ensuring healthy supplies, even of the Motorsport designed and branded items. The only 'problem' model in this respect is probably the ultra-rare M1, but even here there are few worries.

With such specialized cars as these, it is always worthwhile obtaining independent advice. The safest method of purchase is to buy from a specialist who will give you a warranty, but in all cases it is advisable to splash out on an engineer's report: this should pick up a number of points you are likely to overlook and represent money extremely well spent. You should also take care to ensure that the car is precisely what it is claimed to be. Regrettably, fakes are not unknown, and the possibility of forged documents, clocking and even repaired write-offs should always be borne in mind.

M1

The legendary M1 – the first Motorsport-badged BMW and the only true supercar that BMW has ever sold – is a rarified and exotic beast. Since only 450 were ever built (and probably 100 of those are genuine or converted track cars), examples rarely if ever come up for sale, and even if one does, you will probably be asked to pay comfortably more than the list price of the most expensive new BMW for it. It is a sad fact that many M1s will probably never move a wheel in anger again, since they are stored in private collections.

Perhaps the main attraction of the M1 is that it is a much better bet than other, more fragile, exotica: it boasts far better build quality, greater user-friendliness and superior reliability. It was only built with left-hand drive, of course,

There can be few truly helpful comments to make about buying an M1 since being such a rare car every example

Like any cars, BMW M models often change hands privately, but with so much at stake the potential buyer may well feel that the extra security of purchase offered by a recognized dealer is worth having.

should be treated on its own merits. Most are likely to have some minor bodywork problems like stone-chipped paintwork, a damaged front spoiler, crazing in the glassfibre body and perhaps even some rust in the chassis. Major body-off restoration is feasible because of the separate chassis construction, but it is certainly not an easy task since the bodywork is bonded, as well as riveted, to the chassis. Clutches and brakes tend to wear very rapidly, as do tyres.

The engine is robust, but the cost of a rebuild can be extremely high. Timing chains need to be replaced before 100,000 miles come up (at the same time, the crank sprocket should be renewed). Neglected engines can develop worn piston rings, gasket problems and fluid leaks, and the aluminium cylinder head should be checked for signs of cracking.

The interior should also be in complete and original condition. If not, there may be problems sourcing the right bits (though most of the instruments and switches are BMW 6 Series items). There are a handful of dedicated specialists worldwide who know the M1 intimately, and it is to one of these concerns that a thoroughbred car of this rarity should be entrusted to carry out any serious remedial work.

M3 (E30)
Of all the M cars made by BMW, the first-series M3 is the most accessible and certainly one of the most rewarding. It is practical to own, extremely enjoyable in every sense of the word, and a true motoring legend. Price-wise, used examples are now well within the reach of the average enthusiast. Although availability is limited, the choice is wide enough to encompass buying privately or finding a warranted car from a specialist.

Although fewer than 300 old-shape M3s were officially imported to the UK, since the total build approached 18,000, you are equally – if not more – likely to come across an unofficial personal import. Such imports have no less value than the officially imported BMW GB stock, but you do need to be sure that the car is a genuine M3, that it was made in the year stated and that its history is fully documented.

Some identification features should be noted: chassis number sequences are quite complicated but are summarized below:

M3 non-cat (Sep 1986-Feb 1987) – 0842001 to 0845000
M3 non-cat (Feb 1987-Jan 1989) – 2190001 to 2192224
M3 non-cat (Jan-Jul 1989) – AE31000 to AE31242
M3 cat (Sep 1986-Jan 1989) – 1891001 to 1894694
M3 cat (Jan-May 1989) – AE40000 to AE40899
M3 cat (Sep 1989-Dec 1990) – AE40900 to AE42418
M3 cat USA (1986-88) – 2195001 to 2198685
M3 cat USA (Jan 1989-Dec 1990) – AE33000 to AE34628
M3 Evo I (Feb-May 1987) – 2190005 to 2190787
M3 Evo II (Mar-May 1988) – 2191372 to 2191953
M3 Evo III (Jan-Mar 1990) – AC79000 to AC79599
M3 Cabrio non-cat (May-Dec 1988) – 2385001 to 2385042
M3 Cabrio non-cat (Jan-Jun 1989) – EB85000 to EB85093
M3 Cabrio cat (Oct-Dec 1988) – 3559001 to 3559088
M3 Cabrio cat (Jan-Jul 1989) – EB86000 to EB86085
M3 Cabrio cat (Mar 1990-Jul 1991) – EB86086 to EB86561

The Evo I is identifiable by a letter 'E' stamped on to the cast eye of the cylinder head, as well as modified spoilers; but it is not worth any more than a standard M3. The more interesting Evo II can be identified by its white valve cover and air collector box with Motorsport stripes and modified 220bhp engine. The ultra-desirable Evo III is easily recognizable by its 2.5-litre engine, adjustable front and rear spoiler lips, suede steering wheel and gear-knob and unique seats, and its rarity and allure make it the most expensive of the E30 M3 family.

The 1988 Europa Meister special edition was not imported to the UK, but should have a Roberto Ravaglia-signed plaque and extra leather. UK buyers were offered a Roberto Ravaglia limited edition (of 25) in 1989, which again has the signed plaque on the centre console, plus a body-coloured rocker cover and air collector, silver-coloured interior and red or silver paint. Continental customers had the same car, but signed by Johnny Cecotto.

Variations on a theme, in this case a 3 Series line-up. Wheels are not the only visual variable between one model and another, and it takes patience to learn and digest the subtleties of BMW's seemingly ever-changing specification sheets.

The extremely rare M3 Cabriolets have an electric folding roof.

The old-shape M3 was only ever built in left-hand-drive form and, while right-hand-drive conversions do exist, they tend to use the slower 325i steering rack; this might make the M3 easier to live with, but as it negates so much of the car's enjoyment it is better avoided. Also, cars so fitted are worth significantly less. You must be sure that your M3 has the correct specification. Owners often alter things like wheels, door mirrors, interior trim and, most significantly of all, the engine, notably swapping chips in the engine management system. The best advice is to avoid cars which have been tampered with.

Running costs must be addressed with any BMW M car. Insurance ratings are all towards the highest category, and if you are under 25, you can virtually forget about insuring an M3. Fuel economy is reasonable, but original BMW parts are expensive and franchised dealer servicing also works out pretty costly. However, always make sure that any spares you fit are BMW original parts and correct for the specialized M3. An alarm/immobilizer is essential because the M3 is a very attractive item to joy-riders and thieves.

Never consider a car unless it has a full service history. Note also that although M3s are equipped with a service interval indicator light, it is all too easy for a negligent owner to bypass this, and the board which operates it often fails. Always check with a national agency to see if the car has previously been a write-off or has been stolen. Look carefully for signs of accident damage: poor panel fit, filler or mastic between panel joins, evidence of welded repairs, overspray from repainted panels, a feeling that the car does not run straight and true are all warning signs. Also consider that the recorded mileage might have been tampered with.

Problem areas include the gearbox (worn synchromesh, notably on second gear), suspension (dirty and worn seals, 'shot' dampers), faulty air conditioning, tyre wear, kerbed alloy wheels, engine oil and coolant leaks, sometimes severely worn brake pads and discs, slipping clutches (often caused by taking off in second gear rather than the dogleg first), power steering pump leaks, electrical gremlins, faulty instruments, broken seats and loose or missing interior trim.

Home-fitted hi-fi systems can also play havoc with the existing wiring loom.

Bodywork of a misused M3 can suffer from a multitude of scratches and dents, the result of over-enthusiastic driving and the blind offside, and a certain amount of surface rust is not unknown. The engine can also go out of tune and feel flat, usually because the throttle butterflies are out of synch. But despite all the above, generally the M3's mechanical side is very robust since most of the components are genuinely race-proven.

M3 (E36)

Of all the M cars sold in Britain, by far the most common is the new-shape M3. Yet even this model is still comparatively rare: at the time of writing, fewer than 5,000 right-hand-drive cars have been imported to the UK.

The old-shape E30 was really the last of its kind: a car designed by Motorsport engineers with virtually every component different from the 325i. The next-generation E36 M3 is a rather different beast, more of an all-rounder based on the 325i and certainly not an out-and-out homologation racer. The E36, therefore, is an easier car to live with, but ultimately less rewarding. It has right-hand drive and is also much more forgiving, much easier to drive and far more refined. In short, it really appeals to a different sort of driver.

Many of the E30 M3 comments apply to the new-shape M3. It is vital that the car should have a full service record, preferably BMW-stamped, although well-known non-franchised specialists can, at a push, be regarded as an acceptable substitute in this instance. Beware of 'clocked' cars (the electronic odometer does not beat the determined criminal), and cases of forged documentation are not unknown. Look for evidence of previous accidents or vandalism. Broken or missing items (for example damaged locks) can be costly to fix. Once again, always check for any history of theft or outstanding finance.

Although parts, servicing and insurance can be prohibitively expensive, for a performance car of the M3's capabilities, running costs are extremely reasonable. Fuel economy, for example, is outstanding. Values are affected

The all-round appeal of the E36 version of the M3 has considerably widened the market for M cars. But being so liberally endowed with sophisticated equipment, second-hand examples should be treated with extreme caution unless they have an exemplary service record and preferably a history which is known to a conveniently located specialist dealer.

by such capricious influences as colour and options: that violet leather interior might have seemed fashionable to the first owner, but it makes resale more difficult.

Perhaps the main concern with the M3 is its complexity. Far more so than the previous-generation M3, the E36 is a showcase for electronic wizardry. You'll need to check that everything works: the heated mirrors, locks and washers, the sophisticated 750i-derived check control system, on-board computer and options such as air conditioning, cruise control and electrically adjustable and heated front seats. The Cabriolet is still more complex in this respect, with its electric soft-top, electric rear windows and automatic roll-over protection system. Also, the condition of a Cabriolet's interior is much more critical because of its exposure to the elements.

Mechanically, the M3 is extremely tough, but you will need to be sure about the state of the engine's tune: it should pull very strongly in all rev-bands. If it doesn't, there may be a problem with the variable cam timing system or, worse, a gremlin in the electronic management system.

Beware of engines with modified chips (for instance, those which do away with the BMW-limited 155mph top speed).

Post-July 1995 Evolution models, with their six-speed gearbox, carry a significant premium, but the Touring Car-style Sequential M Gearbox does not – it's really a gimmick and should be considered only if you fancy an automatic M3, because this is the closest you'll get. The Convertible certainly carries a premium over both the saloon and the Coupe; the latter pair have broad parity in terms of value.

Areas of concern include excessive brake wear, expensive tyre wear and kerbed wheels, power steering leaks, grounded front spoilers and stone-chipped and scratched paintwork. Check that the car still has the correct specification: the right wheels and tyres, the unique seats and special interior trim. Again avoid modified cars, unless they have verifiable provenance from a BMW-approved modification firm like AC Schnitzer or Alpina.

M535i (E12)
The earliest 'popular' BMW M car was the 1980-81 M535i,

based on the E12 5 Series. In most respects it used standard BMW parts, and is therefore quite practical to run.

The engine is quite serviceable since it is identical to that in the 635CSi. Likewise, the gearbox comes from the 528i, albeit with a different final-drive ratio, and all the suspension – apart from stiffer dampers – is standard 5 Series. Special M parts need to be identified as genuine: the 6.5in wide alloy wheels, optional front airdam/boot spoiler, four Recaro seats and the expensive-to-source M1 steering wheel.

Rust is the deadly enemy of any E12 5 Series, and the M535i does not escape. The only consolation is that most surviving cars will have been well looked after, and probably restored at least once; in any event, you will need to be careful that rust has not compromised the car's structure. Check especially inside the front wings, the windscreen base, floorpan, doors, wheelarches, valances and boot floor.

Your main problem with the M535i will be finding one: only around 200 right-hand-drive cars came to the UK, and such examples as remain are sought-after and usually expensive.

M535i and M5 (E28)

The E28 M535i will only be mentioned in passing because it is not a true M car in the same vein as all other models described in this book. Don't be fooled by its skirts-and-spoilers looks: this is virtually the only difference between an M535i and a standard 535i. Thus it has a standard 3.5-litre engine, standard 528i gearbox, virtually standard suspension, and so on. The only reason why values are so much higher than for normal examples of the 535i is the associations of the letter M. It is also very easy to create an M535i from a standard 535i by sourcing parts off-the-shelf, so beware.

Far more interesting for the enthusiast is the first-generation M5, also based on the E28 bodyshell. This is an entirely different proposition, a hand-built Motorsport car with many features unique to this model. First among these is the M1/M635CSi engine (see comments under M1), plus uprated brakes and steering, reinforced gearbox and special ABS. Like all M models, the M5 tends to be driven hard,

therefore all the mechanicals should be checked for condition.

The M5's interior was subtle but unique. If anything is missing, it will be awkward and expensive to replace it, so tick off the following items: velour carpets on the floor, doors and parcel shelf, Highland fabric for the door inserts and seats, 'M' branded rev-counter, 'M5' badges on the sill kickplates, electrically adjustable BMW sports seats, a leather-bound M Sports steering wheel, and Motorsport colours on the wheel, seats and gear-knob. The exterior should have unique wide BBS alloys, 225/55 tyres, a deeper front spoiler, body-coloured mirrors and M5 badges.

The 1986-87 E28 M5 is extremely rare: only 187 were sold in the UK. When bought new, owners generally used them as everyday transport, so high mileages are common – and the M5 can take it, though you should budget for rebuilding certain parts after about 100,000 miles: for example, a rebuilt head, fresh timing chains and crank sprocket, new suspension balljoints, bushes and diff mountings. Properly cared-for engines can run as far as 200,000 miles. The usual BMW synchromesh problems can be expected, as well as a sloppy gear linkage (due to worn bushes). Brake discs and pads get a pounding, as do tyres, and the ABS needs to be checked carefully. Electrics are another area of concern, especially the air conditioning, sunroof and electrically-adjustable seats. Conversely, the bodywork should pose no problems.

M5 (E34)

More mature than the previous M5, the 1988-95 incarnation makes a fabulous used car buy. Compared with the old M5, it is more efficient, faster, better looking and much more refined, though the trade-off is a less involving drive. If you want obsessively understated looks, yet supercar-slaying ability, the M5 has no peers – and it seats five in superb comfort. Again this was a hand-built machine, utterly exclusive and, as a used car, extremely desirable.

British buyers did not have the chance to buy an M5 until February 1990 and it is an extremely rare sight, so used examples are expensive and sought-after. One cast-iron rule is never to touch a car without a seamless, impeccable

When examining a used M car, pay particular attention to the condition of the interior, especially the upholstery and door trim, which is likely to be far more expensive to renovate or replace than removing a few 'battle scars' from the exterior bodywork.

service history, fully BMW dealer-stamped. Some owners are bound to take a short-cut on servicing since it is so expensive, so make sure you have the means to run an M5 (insurance and parts are very expensive). Make the usual checks about authenticity and history, and be suspicious of any car with more than a couple of owners from new. Accident damage is not at all uncommon, and evidence of repairs needs to be searched out with diligence.

The engine is M1-derived, but far more complex (consider the variable-length inlet valving, six separate throttles, hot-wire induction metering and secondary catalyst fan): there's much more to go wrong. The condition of the rear suspension bushes is critical to the car's handling. The clever finned 17in alloy wheels of the original M5 are expensive to replace if badly kerbed, as are the tyres. Just about everything is electronically-controlled (such as the self-levelling rear suspension, ventilation and self-diagnostic system), so beware of any glitches, which could indicate big trouble in store. Things became even more complex after the 1992 evolution (3.8-litre engine, six individual ignition

coils, automatic adaptive suspension). A six-speed gearbox was introduced in 1994, alongside novel two-piece 'floating' disc brakes.

Specification plays an important role: leather is preferable, white is the worst colour, and electrically adjustable front and rear seats are useful, but potentially troublesome. Beware of kitsch kitted-out M5s and cars with purple paintwork, dechromed brightwork and a rear spoiler.

M635CSi
Although in production from 1983, the UK did not receive the right-hand-drive M635CSi until 1985. That means it is yet another M rarity, which seldom comes up for sale. Examples may be sought-after, but used prices can be very reasonable – certainly within the M3 category – mainly because the perceived cost of ownership is so high. The M635CSi was the *autobahnstormer* of the BMW range in the 1980s and that role is still relevant today. The enhanced M1 engine is as effective as ever.

Cylinder bores can wear at around 100,000 miles, so rev

Because of its style and rarity, the 635CSi has to be one of the most coveted of all the BMW M cars. From time to time they are offered for sale comparatively cheaply, but before rushing for your cheque book remember that the cost of ownership only begins with the purchase of the car. Periodic maintenance and service tends not to come cheaply with this model.

the engine to 4,500rpm for 15 seconds and then back off: a puff of smoke indicates worn valve guides and seals, but a billowing plume means worn bores. Camshafts tend to wear around the 90,000-mile mark, or sooner if not properly serviced; listen for noise from the front of the cam, since such noises can become very expensive. A whining sound from the gearbox will usually mean having to replace it.

Rust is a major worry on all 6 Series models, although by 1984 BMW had most of the problems under control. Corrosion attacks the front wings and, crucially, the strut and rear subframe mountings. The sunroof and windscreen seals are also prone to leaking.

Electrical problems are ever-present, and there are a lot of gizmos on the M635CSi. For instance, on post-1987 cars there are standard electrically-adjustable leather front seats,

and all cars have electronic heating control, a troublesome active check system and an on-board computer. Be prepared to budget on spending a good sum replacing regular items like suspension bushes, steering joints, idler bushes, dampers, track rods and brake discs. If the clutch seems unduly heavy, it may mean simply a new hose, on the other hand the diaphragm may be worn through over-use, in which case a new clutch will be needed. Pre-September 1987 cars should have split-rim alloy wheels (they were one-piece thereafter) and their condition should be checked carefully because replacing them will be very expensive; also, bear in mind the considerable cost of replacement tyres. Finally, when choosing a car, remember that leather upholstery is preferable to cloth, which wears rapidly and costs a lot to replace.

APPENDIX A

Technical specifications

M1

Produced Feb 1979-Jul 1981.

Engine: In-line 6-cylinder, iron block and aluminium DOHC 24-valve cylinder head. 93.4x84mm, 3,453cc, compression ratio 9.0:1. Kugelfischer-Bosch fuel injection. 277bhp at 6,500rpm, 239lb.ft at 5,000rpm.

Transmission: Mid-engine, rear drive. Final drive 4.22:1, 40% limited-slip differential. Gear ratios: 1st, 2.42; 2nd, 1.61; 3rd, 1.14; 4th, 0.85; 5th 0.70:1.

Suspension, steering and brakes: IFS, coil springs, height-adjustable telescopic dampers, MacPherson struts, lower wishbones, anti-roll bar. IRS, coil springs, trailing arms, height-adjustable telescopic dampers, anti-roll bar. Rack-and-pinion steering (3.2 turns lock-to-lock), unassisted. Servo-assisted 300mm/11.8in vented front discs, 297mm/11.7in vented rear discs.

Wheels and tyres: Campagnolo alloy 7x16in front and 8x16in rear wheels with 205/55 VR16 front and 225/50 VR16 rear tyres.

Body: 2-door coupe in plastic.

Dimensions: Length 4,361mm/171.7in, wheelbase 2,560mm/100.8in, width 1,824mm/71.8in, height 1,140mm/44.9in, kerb weight 1,300kg/2,867lb.

Number produced: 450.

UK retail price: Equivalent of £37,500 in 1979.

M3 (E30)

Produced Sep 1986-Dec 1990.

Engine: In-line 4-cylinder, iron block and aluminium DOHC 16-valve cylinder head. 93.4x84mm, 2,302cc, compression ratio 10.5:1. Bosch ML Motronic fuel injection/ignition. 200bhp at 6,750rpm (195bhp with catalyst), 176lb.ft at 4,750rpm (169lb.ft with catalyst).

Transmission: Front engine, rear drive. Final drive 3.25:1, 25% limited-slip differential. Gear ratios: 1st, 3.72; 2nd, 2.40; 3rd, 1.77; 4th, 1.26; 5th 1.00:1.

Suspension, steering and brakes: IFS, coil springs, Boge gas dampers, MacPherson struts, trailing arms, anti-roll bar. IRS, coil springs, trailing arms, Boge gas dampers, anti-roll bar. Rack-and-pinion steering (19.6:1 ratio), power-assisted, LHD only. Servo-assisted 284mm/11.18in vented front discs, 250mm/9.84in rear discs, ABS.

Wheels and tyres: Alloy BBS 7x15in wheels with 205/55 VR15 tyres.

Body: 2-door saloon in steel, with plastic front bumper/spoiler, bootlid, rear bumper and sills.

Dimensions: Length 4,360mm/171.7in, wheelbase 2,562mm/100.9in, width 1,675mm/65.9in, height 1,365mm/53.7in, kerb weight 1,200kg/2,640lb.

Number produced: 17,184 (all M3 saloons).

UK retail price: £22,750 in 1987.

M3 (215bhp version)

Produced Sep 1989-Dec 1990. All details as M3 except:

Engine: 215bhp at 6,750rpm, 170lb.ft at 4,600rpm.

Suspension: Optional Boge electronic damping.

M3 Cabriolet (E30)

Produced May 1988-Jun 1991. All details as M3 except:

Engine: 200bhp engine available from May 1988 to Jun 1989, 195bhp catalysed engine available from Oct 1988 to Jun 1989, 215bhp catalysed engine available from Mar 1990 to Jun 1991. Details in relevant sections above.

Body: 2-door convertible.

Dimensions: Length 4,345mm/171in, height 1,370mm/53.9in, kerb weight 1,360kg/2,998lb.

Number produced: 786.

UK retail price: £37,250 in 1989.

M3 Evolution I

Produced Feb-May 1987. All details as M3.

Number produced: 505.

M3 Evolution II

Produced Mar-May 1988. All details as M3 except:

Engine: Compression ratio 11.0:1, 220bhp at 6,750rpm, 181lb.ft at 4,750rpm.

Transmission: Final drive 3.15:1.

Wheels and tyres: 7.5x16in BBS alloy wheels with 225/45 ZR16 tyres.

Number produced: 501.

UK retail price: £26,960.

M3 Europa Meister 88

Produced Oct-Nov 1988. All details as M3 (catalyst).
Number produced: 150.
UK retail price: Not sold in UK.

M3 Cecotto/Ravaglia

Produced Apr-Jul 1989. All details as M3 (215bhp version) except:
Wheels and tyres: 7.5x16in BBS alloy wheels with 225/45 ZR16 tyres.
Number produced: 505.
UK retail price: £26,850.

M3 Sport Evolution III

Produced Dec 1989-Mar 1990. All details as M3 except:
Engine: 95x87mm, 2,467cc, compression ratio 10.2:1. 238bhp at 7,000rpm, 177lb.ft at 4,750rpm.
Transmission: Final drive 3.15:1.
Wheels and tyres: 7.5x16in alloy wheels with 225/45 ZR16 tyres.
Number produced: 600.
UK retail price: £34,500

M3 Coupe 3.0 (E36)

Produced Oct 1992-Jul 1995.
Engine: In-line 6-cylinder, iron block and aluminium DOHC 24-valve cylinder head. 86x85.8mm, 2,990cc, compression ratio 10.8:1. Bosch Motronic 3.3 fuel injection. 286bhp at 7,000rpm, 236lb.ft at 3,600rpm.
Transmission: Front engine, rear drive. Final drive 3.15:1, 25% limited-slip differential. Gear ratios: 1st, 4.20; 2nd, 2.49; 3rd, 1.66; 4th, 1.24; 5th, 1.00:1.
Suspension, steering and brakes: IFS, single joint spring strut axle, coil springs and dampers, anti-roll bar. IRS, central arm axle with longitudinal control arm and double track control arm, coil springs and dampers, anti-roll bar. Rack-and-pinion steering (16.8:1 ratio), power-assisted. Servo-assisted 315mm/12.4in vented front discs, 313mm/12.3in vented rear discs, ABS.
Wheels and tyres: Alloy 7.5x17in with 235/40 ZR17 tyres, optional 8.5x17in rear wheels with 245/40 ZR17 tyres.
Body: 2-door coupe in steel.
Dimensions: Length 4,433mm/174.5in, wheelbase 2,700mm/106.3in, width 1,710mm/67.3in, height 1,366mm/53.8in, kerb weight 1,460kg/3,219lb.
Number produced: 25,755.
UK retail price: £32,450 in 1993.

M3 Cabriolet 3.0 (E36)

Produced Jan 1994-Jul 1995. Details as M3 Coupe (E36) except:
Wheels and tyres: Alloy 7.5x17in front, 8.5x17in rear wheels with 235/40 ZR17 tyres.
Body: 2-door convertible.
Dimensions: Wheelbase 2,696mm/106.1in, height 1,348mm/53.1in, kerb weight 1,540kg/3,395lb.
Number produced: 1,975.
UK retail price: £38,210 in 1994.

M3 Saloon 3.0 (E36)

Produced Jun 1994-Jul 1995. Details as M3 Coupe (E36) except:
Wheels and tyres: Alloy 7.5x17in front, 8.5x17in rear wheels with 235/40 ZR17 tyres.
Body: 4-door saloon.
Dimensions: Wheelbase 2,710mm/106.7in, height 1,365mm/53.7in.
Number produced: 1,303.

M3 GT (E36)

Produced Jan-May 1995. Details as M3 Coupe (E36) except:
Engine: 295bhp at 7,000rpm, 238lb.ft at 3,900rpm.
Number produced: 396.
UK retail price: Not sold in UK.

M3 Evolution Coupe (E36)

Produced Oct 1995-date. Details as M3 (E36) except:
Engine: 86.4x91mm, 3,201cc, compression ratio 11.3:1. 321bhp at 7,400rpm, 258lb.ft at 3,250rpm.
Transmission: Final drive 3.23:1. Gear ratios: 1st, 4.23; 2nd, 2.51; 3rd, 1.67; 4th, 1.23; 5th, 1.00, 6th, 0.83:1.
Suspension, steering and brakes: 315mm/12.4in vented front discs, 312mm/12.3in vented rear discs.
Wheels and tyres: Alloy 7.5x17in front wheels with 225/45 ZR17 tyres, 8.5x17in rear wheels with 245/40 ZR17 tyres.
Dimensions: Wheelbase 2,710mm/106.7in.
Number produced: 7,556 by end of 1996.
UK retail price: £36,550 in 1996.

M3 Evolution Saloon (E36)

Produced Nov 1995-date. Details as M3 Evolution Coupe (E36) except:
Body: 4-door saloon.
Dimensions: Width 1,698mm/66.9in, height 1,365mm/53.7in.
Number produced: 3,906 by end of 1996.

M3 Evolution Cabriolet (E36)

Produced Feb 1996-date. Details as M3 Evolution Coupe (E36) except:
Body: 2-door convertible.
Dimensions: Height 1,340mm/52.75in, kerb weight 1,560kg/3,439lb.
Number produced: 1,254 by end of 1996.
UK retail price: £41,800 in 1996.

M535i (E12)

Produced Apr 1980-May 1981
Engine: In-line 6-cylinder, iron block and aluminium DOHC 16-valve cylinder head. 93.4x84mm, 3,453cc, compression ratio 9.3:1. Bosch L-Jetronic fuel injection. 218bhp at 5,200rpm, 228lb.ft at 4,000rpm.
Transmission: Front engine, rear drive. Final drive 3.07:1 or 3.25:1, 25% limited-slip differential. Gear ratios: 1st, 3.72; 2nd, 2.40; 3rd, 1.77; 4th, 1.24; 5th, 1.01:1.
Suspension, steering and brakes: IFS, coil springs, telescopic dampers, MacPherson struts, auxiliary rubber springs, lower wishbones, lower trailing links, anti-roll bar. IRS, coil springs, semi-trailing arms, telescopic dampers, auxiliary rubber springs, anti-roll bar. Worm-and-roller steering, servo-assisted. Servo-assisted 280mm/11in vented front discs, 272mm/10.7in rear discs.
Wheels and tyres: Alloy BBS 6.5x14in wheels with 195/70 VR14 tyres.
Body: 4-door saloon in steel.
Dimensions: Length 4,620mm/181.9in, wheelbase 2,636mm/103.8in, width 1,690mm/66.5in, height 1,425mm/56.1in, kerb weight 1,450kg/3,197lb.
Number produced: 1,410 + 240 CKD.
UK retail price: £13,745 in 1980.

M535i (E28)

Produced Oct 1984-Dec 1987.
Engine: In-line 6-cylinder, iron block and aluminium DOHC 24-valve cylinder head. 92x86mm, 3,430cc, compression ratio 10:1 (8:1 with catalyst). Bosch Motronic fuel injection. 218bhp at 5,200rpm (185bhp at 5,400rpm with catalyst), 229lb.ft at 4,000rpm (210lb.ft with catalyst).
Transmission: Front engine, rear drive. Final drive 3.25 or 3.07:1, 25% limited-slip differential. Gear ratios: 1st, 3.82; 2nd, 2.20; 3rd, 1.40; 4th, 1.00; 5th, 0.81:1. Optional ZF automatic with 3.45:1 final drive, gear ratios: 1st, 2.48; 2nd, 1.48; 3rd, 1.00; 4th, 0.73:1.
Suspension, steering and brakes: IFS, coil springs, MacPherson struts, transverse links, Bilstein gas-filled telescopic dampers, anti-roll bar. IRS, coil springs, semi-trailing arms, Bilstein gas-filled telescopic dampers, anti-roll bar. ZF recirculating-ball steering (15.1:1 ratio), power-assisted. Servo-assisted 284mm/11.2in front discs, 284mm/11.2in rear discs, ABS.
Wheels and tyres: Alloy 165x390 wheels with 220/55 VR390 tyres.
Body: 4-door saloon in steel.
Dimensions: Length 4,620mm/181.9in, wheelbase 2,625mm/103.4in, width 1,700mm/66.9in, height 1,397mm/55in, kerb weight 1,450kg/3,197lb.
Number produced: 9,483.
UK retail price: £17,950 in 1985.

M5 (E28)

Produced Oct 1984-Dec 1987.
Engine: In-line 6 cylinder, iron block and aluminium DOHC 24-valve cylinder head. 93.4x84mm, 3,453cc, compression ratio 10.5:1 (9.8:1 in USA). Bosch Motronic fuel injection. 286bhp at 6,500rpm (256bhp in USA), 250lb.ft at 4,500rpm (243lb.ft in USA).
Transmission: Front engine, rear drive. Final drive 3.73:1, 25% limited-slip differential. Gear ratios: 1st, 3.51; 2nd, 2.08; 3rd, 1.35; 4th, 1.00; 5th, 0.81:1.
Suspension, steering and brakes: IFS, coil springs, MacPherson struts, transverse links, Bilstein gas-filled telescopic dampers, anti-roll bar. IRS, coil springs, semi-trailing arms, Bilstein gas-filled telescopic dampers, anti-roll bar. ZF recirculating-ball steering (15.1:1 ratio), power-assisted. Servo-assisted 284mm/11.2in vented front discs, 284mm/11.2in solid rear discs, ABS.
Wheels and tyres: BBS 165x390mm alloy wheels with 220/55 VR390 tyres.
Body: 4-door saloon in steel.
Dimensions: Length 4,620mm/181.9in, wheelbase 2,625mm/103.4in, width 1,700mm/66.9in, height 1,397mm/55in, kerb weight 1,470kg/3,240lb.
Number produced: 2,145 + 96 CKD.
UK retail price: £31,295 in 1986.

M5 (E34) 3.5

Produced Sep 1988-Mar 1993.
Engine: In-line 6-cylinder, iron block and aluminium DOHC 24-valve cylinder head. 93.4x86mm, 3,535cc, compression ratio 10.0:1. Bosch fuel injection. 315bhp at 6,900rpm (310bhp in USA), 266lb.ft at 4,750rpm.
Transmission: Front engine, rear drive. Final drive 3.91:1, 25% limited-slip differential. Gear ratios: 1st, 3.51; 2nd, 2.08; 3rd, 1.35; 4th, 1.00; 5th, 0.81:1.
Suspension, steering and brakes: IFS, coil springs, MacPherson

struts, Bilstein telescopic dampers, 25mm anti-roll bar. IRS, coil springs, semi-trailing arms, auxiliary pivot link, Bilstein telescopic dampers, 18mm anti-roll bar. Recirculating-ball steering (15.64:1 ratio), speed-variable power-assisted. Servo-assisted 315mm/12.4in vented front discs, 300mm/11.8in solid rear discs.
Wheels and tyres: Alloy 8x17in wheels with 235/45 ZR17 tyres, optional 9x17in wheels with 255/40 ZR17 tyres.
Body: 4-door saloon in steel.
Dimensions: Length 4,720mm/186in, wheelbase 2,761mm/108.7in, width 1,751mm/68.9in, height 1,392mm/54.8in, kerb weight 1,670kg/3,682lb.
Number produced: 8,079 + 265 CKD.
UK retail price: £43,465 in 1990.

M5 3.8 Saloon
Produced Dec 1991-Jul 1995. Details as M5 (E34) except:
Engine: 94.6x90mm, 3,795cc, compression ratio 10.5:1. 340bhp at 6,900rpm, 295lb.ft at 4,750rpm.
Transmission: From May 1994: 6-speed manual gearbox, final drive 3.23:1. Gear ratios: 1st, 4.23; 2nd, 2.52; 3rd, 1.66; 4th, 1.22; 5th, 1.00; 6th, 0.83:1.
Suspension, steering and brakes: Automatically adaptive Boge dampers, optional Nürburgring suspension with 1mm thicker rear anti-roll bar and regeared steering.
Wheels and tyres: Optional 9x17in rear wheels with 255/40 ZR17 tyres. From 1994: 8x18in front and 9x18in rear wheels fitted with 245/40 ZR18 tyres.
Number produced: 3,014.
UK retail price: £48,950 in 1992.

M5 3.8 Touring
Produced Mar 1992-Jul 1995. Details as M5 3.8 Saloon except:
Wheels and tyres: Standard 9in wide rear wheels with 255/40 ZR17 tyres (1992-94).
Dimensions: Kerb weight 1,730kg/3,814lb.
Number produced: 891.
UK retail price: Not sold in UK.

M635CSi/M6
Produced Apr 1984-Feb 1989.
Engine: In-line 6-cylinder, iron block and aluminium DOHC 24-valve cylinder head. 93.4x84mm, 3,453cc, compression ratio 10.5:1. Bosch L-Jetronic fuel injection. 286bhp at 6,500rpm (260bhp with catalyst), 251lb.ft at 4,500rpm (243lb.ft with catalyst).
Transmission: Front engine, rear drive. Final drive 3.73:1 or 3.91:1, 25% limited-slip differential. Gear ratios: 1st, 3.51; 2nd, 2.08; 3rd, 1.35; 4th, 1.00; 5th, 0.81:1.
Suspension, steering and brakes: IFS, coil springs, MacPherson struts, lower wishbones, anti-roll bar. IRS, coil springs, semi-trailing arms, telescopic dampers, anti-roll bar. Recirculating-ball steering (16.9:1 ratio), power-assisted. Servo-assisted 300mm/11.8in vented front discs, 272mm/10.7in solid rear discs.
Wheels and tyres: Alloy 165x390mm wheels with 220/55 VR390 tyres or 210x415 wheels with 240/45 VR415 tyres (from Sep 87: standard 245/45 VR415 tyres).
Body: 2-door coupe in steel.
Dimensions: Length 4,755mm/187.2in, wheelbase 2,625mm/103.3in, width 1,725mm/67.9in, height 1,353mm/53.2in, kerb weight 1,510kg/3,329lb.
Number produced: 5,855.
UK retail price: £32,195 in 1985.

M Roadster
Produced Mar 1997-date.
Engine: In-line 6-cylinder, iron block and aluminium DOHC 24-valve cylinder head. 86.4x91mm, 3,201cc, compression ratio 11.3:1, fuel injection. 321bhp at 7,400rpm, 258lb.ft at 3,250rpm.
Transmission: Front engine, rear drive. Final drive 3.15:1. Gear ratios: 1st, 4.20; 2nd, 2.49; 3rd, 1.66; 4th, 1.24; 5th 1.00:1.
Suspension, steering and brakes: IFS, coil springs, MacPherson struts, lower wishbones, anti-roll bar. IRS, coil springs, semi-trailing arms, telescopic dampers, anti-roll bar. Rack-and-pinion steering (17.8:1 ratio), power-assisted. Servo-assisted 315mm/12.4in vented front discs, 312mm/12.3in vented rear discs.
Wheels and tyres: Alloy 7.5x17in front wheels with 225/45 ZR17 tyres, 9x17in rear wheels with 245/40 ZR17 tyres.
Body: 2-door convertible in steel.
Dimensions: Length 4,025mm/158.5in, wheelbase 2,459mm/96.8in, width 1,740mm/68.5in, height 1,266mm/49.8in, kerb weight 1,350kg/2,976lb.
Number produced: Still in production.
UK retail price: Not yet on sale at time of writing (estimated £40,000).

Production figures

The year-by-year production figures were supplied direct from BMW M GmbH. UK import figures are the totals of official UK registrations, as recorded by BMW (GB), and do not include 'grey' imports.

Note:
CKD = Complete Knocked Down
SKD = Semi Knocked Down

M1 (Feb 1979-Jul 1981)

1979	144
1980	251
1981	55
Total:	450

M3 (Sep 1986-Jul 1991) (E30)

	M3 Saloon (Sep 86-Dec 90)		M3 Convertible (May 88-Jul 91)	
		UK imports		UK imports
1986	2,397			
1987	6,396	55		
1988	3,426	58	130	
1989	2,541	62	180	19
1990	2,424	36	176	13
1991		25	300	1
1992		21		
Total prod:	17,184	257	786	33

NB. Above totals include the following:
Evolution I, Feb-May 1987 – prod: 505 *(7 UK imports)*
Evolution II, Mar-May 1988 – prod: 501 *(51 UK imports)*
Evolution III, Dec 1989-Mar 1990 – prod: 600 *(45 UK imports)*
Europa Meister 88, Oct-Nov 1988 – prod: 150 *(no UK imports)*
Ravaglia/Cecotto, Apr-Jul 1989 – prod: 505 *(25 UK imports)*

M3 (Oct 1992-date) (E36)

	M3 Coupe 3.0 (Oct 92-Jul 95)			M3 Cabriolet 3.0 (Jan 94-Jul 95)		M3 Saloon 3.0 (Jun 94-Jul 95)	
		SKD	UK imports		UK imports		UK imports
1992	470	50					
1993	6,080	632	270				
1994	9,289	66	789	1,121	210	288	
1995	9,168		687	854	333	1,015	389
1996			6		1		2
Total:	25,007	748	1,752	1,975	544	1,303	391

Note: The Coupe total includes 396 GT models produced between January and May 1995 (no UK imports)

	M3 Evo Coupe (Oct 95-date)	M3 Evo Cabriolet (Feb 96-date)	M3 Evo Saloon (Nov 95-date)	
				UK imports*
1995	660		267	
1996	6,896	1,254	3,639	1,609

Total: All three M3 Evolution models still in production at time of writing

*All M3 Evolution models

M535i (Apr 1980-May 1981) (E12)

		UK imports
1980	919	71
1981	491	335
1982		2
Total:	1,410 + 240 CKD	408

M535i (Oct 1984-Dec 1987) (E28)

		UK imports
1984	31	2
1985	4,826	685
1986	3,523	665
1987	1,103	438
1988		18
Total:	9,483	1,808

M5 (Oct 1984-Jun 1988) (E28)

		CKD	UK imports
1984	25		
1985	267		
1986	478		65
1987	1,375	60	98
1988		36	14
Total Prod:	2,145	96	177

M5 (Sep 1988-Jul 1995) (E34)

	3.5 Saloon Sep 88-Mar 93)		3.8 Saloon (Dec 91-Jul 95)		3.8 Touring (Mar 92-Jul 95)
		CKD			UK imports *
1988	331				
1989	2,339				2
1990	3,022	67			189
1991	2,033	108	120		120
1992	224	90	1,553	446	99
1993	130		643	209	105
1994			483	117	92
1995			215	119	89
Total:	8,079	265	3,014	891	696
Grand total:	12,249				

* No distinction made in the import figures between M5 models;
no examples of M5 Touring were imported

M635CSi/M6 (Apr 1984 to Feb 1989)

		UK imports
1984	1,412	
1985	1,763	209
1986	704	108
1987	1,487	54
1988	437	36
1989	52	54
1990		13
1991		3
Total:	5,855	477

850CSi (Aug 1992-Dec 1996)

1992	208
1993	586
1994	419
1995	220
1996	77
Total:	1,510

APPENDIX C

Performance figures for M cars

M1

Quoted bhp	277
Maximum (mph)	162
0-30mph (sec)	2.1
0-40mph	3.1
0-50mph	4.1
0-60mph	5.5
0-70mph	6.8
0-80mph	8.9
0-90mph	10.9
0-100mph	13.0
0-110mph	16.6
0-120mph	20.2
Standing ¼-mile	13.6
50-70mph (top)	8.4
Overall mpg	17.0
Kerb weight (kg)	1,418
Source/date *Autocar* 9/80	

M3 E30 Saloon

Quoted bhp	200	200
Maximum (mph)	140	143
0-30mph (sec)	2.8	2.3
0-40mph	3.9	3.4
0-50mph	5.5	5.3
0-60mph	7.1	6.8
0-70mph	9.5	9.2
0-80mph	11.9	11.5
0-90mph	15.2	15.1
0-100mph	19.0	18.8
0-110mph	23.7	-
0-120mph	29.8	-
Standing ¼-mile	15.7	-
50-70mph (top)	9.4	6.1 (4th)
Overall mpg	20.3	23.0
Kerb weight (kg)	1,252	1,200
Source/date *Autocar* 4/87	*Car* 5/87	

M3 E30 Convertible

Quoted bhp	200
Maximum mph	146
0-30mph (sec)	2.1
0-40mph	2.9
0-50mph	4.7
0-60mph	6.0
0-70mph	8.0
0-80mph	10.7
0-90mph	12.0
0-100mph	16.6
0-110mph	22.5
0-120mph	28.3
Standing ¼-mile	15.8
50-70mph (top)	9.5
Overall mpg	22.2
Kerb weight (kg)	1,411
Source/date *Autocar* 2/89	

M3 E30 Evolution II

Quoted bhp	220
Maximum (mph)	148
0-30mph (sec)	2.5
0-40mph	3.6
0-50mph	5.1
0-60mph	6.6
0-70mph	8.8
0-80mph	11.0
0-90mph	13.9
0-100mph	17.8
0-110mph	21.9
0-120mph	-
Standing ¼-mile	15.2
50-70mph, top	9.8
Overall mpg	26.0
Kerb weight (kg)	1,274
Source/date *Autocar* 9/88	

M3 E30 Evolution III

No comprehensive British road test was ever published but BMW's claims were as follows:

Quoted bhp	238
Maximum (mph)	154
0-60mph (sec)	6.4
Standing km	26.7
Kerb weight (kg)	1,200

M3 Coupe (E36)

Quoted bhp	286
Maximum (mph)	162
0-30mph (sec)	2.2
0-40mph	3.1
0-50mph	4.1
0-60mph	5.4
0-70mph	6.9
0-80mph	8.8
0-90mph	10.8
0-100mph	13.1
0-110mph	16.4
0-120mph	20.0
Standing ¼-mile	13.9
50-70mph (top)	7.1
Overall mpg	26.2
Kerb weight (kg)	1,520
Source/date *Autocar* 8/93	

M3 Convertible (E36)

Quoted bhp	286
Maximum (mph)	155
0-30mph (sec)	2.3
0-40mph	3.3
0-50mph	4.5
0-60mph	5.7
0-70mph	7.4
0-80mph	9.4
0-90mph	11.6
0-100mph	14.3
0-110mph	-
0-120mph	-
Standing ¼-mile	14.4
50-70mph (top)	7.7
Overall mpg	22.7
Kerb weight (kg)	1,580
Source/date *Autocar* 7/94	

M3 Saloon (E36)
Quoted bhp	286
Maximum (mph)	156
0-30mph (sec)	2.3
0-60mph	5.5
0-100mph	14.4
Standing ¼-mile	14.3
50-70mph (top)	8.4
Kerb weight (kg)	1,535
Source/date *Autocar* 2/95	

M3 Evolution
No comprehensive British road test published at the time of writing but BMW's claims are as follows:
Quoted bhp	321
Maximum (mph)	155
0-60mph (sec)	5.4
Standing ¼-mile	
50-70mph (top)	
Overall mpg	32.3
Kerb weight (kg)	1,440

M535i (E12)
Quoted bhp	218
Maximum, mph	139
0-30mph, sec	2.4
0-40mph	3.5
0-50mph	5.3
0-60mph	7.1
0-70mph	9.2
0-80mph	11.9
0-90mph	15.7
0-100mph	19.2
0-110mph	24.5
0-120mph	32.2
Standing ¼-mile	15.7
50-70mph (top)	8.0
Overall mpg	20.2
Kerb weight (kg)	1,501
Source/date *Autocar* 8/80	

M535i (E28)
Quoted bhp	218
Maximum (mph)	141
0-30mph	2.8
0-40mph	4.2

0-50mph	5.7
0-60mph	7.4
0-70mph	10.4
0-80mph	12.9
0-90mph	15.8
0-100mph	19.5
0-110mph	24.4
0-120mph	30.8
Standing ¼-mile	15.6
50-70mph (top)	12.3
Overall mpg	17.7
Kerb weight (kg)	1,414
Source/date *Autocar* 1/85	

M5 (E28)
No comprehensive British road test was ever published but BMW's claims were as follows:
Quoted bhp	286
Maximum (mph)	153
0-60mph (sec)	6.2
50-75mph (4th)	7.7
Kerb weight (kg)	1,470

M5 3.5 (E34)
Quoted bhp	315
Maximum (mph)	157
0-30mph (sec)	2.6
0-40mph	3.8
0-50mph	5.1
0-60mph	6.4
0-70mph	8.4
0-80mph	10.5
0-90mph	12.6
0-100mph	15.6
0-110mph	18.8
0-120mph	22.2
Standing ¼-mile	15.0
50-70mph (top)	9.2
Overall mpg	19.0
Kerb weight (kg)	1,670
Source/date *Autocar* 9/90	

M5 3.8 6-speed
Quoted bhp	340
Maximum (mph)	170
0-30mph (sec)	2.0

0-40mph	3.2
0-50mph	4.2
0-60mph	5.4
0-70mph	7.1
0-80mph	8.9
0-90mph	10.9
0-100mph	13.6
0-110mph	16.7
0-120mph	20.0
Standing ¼-mile	14.0
50-70mph (top)	10.4
Overall mpg	16.8
Kerb weight (kg)	1724
Source/date *Autocar* 11/94	

M635CSi
Quoted bhp	286
Maximum (mph)	150
0-30mph (sec)	2.4
0-40mph	3.5
0-50mph	4.6
0-60mph	6.0
0-70mph	7.9
0-80mph	9.9
0-90mph	12.1
0-100mph	15.1
0-110mph	18.4
0-120mph	22.5
Standing ¼-mile	14.6
50-70mph (top)	9.3
Overall mpg	20.6
Kerb weight (kg)	1,570
Source/date *Autocar* 1/89	

M Roadster
No comprehensive British test published at time of writing but BMW's claims are as follows:
Quoted bhp	321
Maximum (mph)	155
0-62mph (sec)	5.4
Standing km	24.4
50-75mph (4th)	5.3
Overall mpg	25.4
Kerb weight (kg)	1,350